THE BETTER BOOK FOR GETTING HIRED

THE BETTER BOOK FOR GETTING HIRED

How to write a great resume, sell yourself in the interview, and get that job

Robert P. Downe

Self-Counsel Press
(a division of)
International Self-Counsel Press Ltd.
Canada U.S.A.

Printed in Canada

First edition: April, 1982
Reprinted: February, 1984; October, 1988
Second edition: February, 1992

Canadian Cataloguing in Publication Data
Downe, Robert P. (Robert Percy), 1952-
The better book for getting hired

(Self-counsel reference series)
ISBN 0-88908-995-7
1. Applications for positions. 2. Résumés
(Employment) 3. Employment interviewing. I. Title.
II. Series.
HF5382.75.C3D69 1991 650.14 C91-091731-0

Self-Counsel Press
(*a division of*)
International Self-Counsel Press Ltd.
Head and Editorial Office
1481 Charlotte Road
North Vancouver, British Columbia V7J 1H1

U.S. Address
1704 N. State Street
Bellingham, Washington 98225

To my wife (Lorraine), mother (Gladys), brother (Rick), and father (Bob) without whose unconditional care, respect and understanding the contents of this work would not have been possible.

CONTENTS

SAMPLES

APPENDIX — SAMPLE RESUMES

INTRODUCTION

This book will show you all the steps you need to follow in order to find and secure meaningful employment. By learning and using the proven job hunting techniques contained in this book, you will be able to successfully market your work related strengths to employers and avoid the common mistakes made by job hunters who use conventional methods.

By conventional methods, I mean the early morning runs to public employment centers that always seem to start out in hopeful expectation and end in despair; the counter-productive conversations with employment counselors and others who are supposed to be experts on the job search; the dedicated reading of newspaper want ads; the countless number of resumes you send off in response to classified ads that fail to even solicit a letter of acknowledgment (despite the amount of hard work you put into it); the tiresome hours spent knocking on the doors of various business establishments hoping some smart employer will finally recognize and appreciate your true employable value; the leisure hours (what few of them you have) spent looking for understanding from friends and family about how hopeless the job hunt seems; and then, of course, what's worst of all — the moments spent blaming yourself for not having what it takes to find and secure meaningful employment.

This is the conventional way of looking for employment and in following it, some job hunters are driven into taking extreme measures. For example, consider the job hunters who hope to find employment by advertising their availability for work in "employment wanted" ads:

- Department store manager requires immediate full-time work. Have 8 yrs. experience. Please call: 333-1234.

- Capable energetic man with extensive experience in contracting, industrial sales and management. Available immediately: 909-0000.

- Young man needs any type of work. Phone David at 777-6543.

- Mechanical engineer desires full-time employment approximately December 11, prefer flat rate work in small shop. Colwood area: 123-4567.

- Young lady requires part-time employment. Experience in banking, posting, retail sales, some bookkeeping experience. Call Carol: 404-4444.

The above employment wanted ads are all examples of what some job hunters will resort to in desperate moments, because they do not know how to effectively market their work related strengths.

Is it possible to secure meaningful employment without having to rely upon conventional methods? The answer to this is a very definite YES. You can say goodbye forever to employment counselors, personnel office people, bureaucrats and any of the other people you normally encounter along the way in your job search. Sound incredible? Well, it's true. There is a better way — a way that is easier on your nerves and much more promising in its results.

And what is the alternative to using conventional job hunting methods, you ask. It is first of all knowing what kind of specific skills, abilities, knowledge, and experience employers are looking for from job applicants; it is knowing how to demonstrate through your resume, in concise, forceful, and easy-to-understand terms, how you meet the requirements of any position you are applying for; it is knowing how to uncover the people with hiring power in the place you would like to work (without having to contact the business itself). In one statement, it is knowing how to market your work related strengths.

In reading this book from cover to cover, you will discover how to do all of the above

and much more. This book is a practical guide for helping the job hunter (regardless of background) secure meaningful employment.

However, it is extremely important that you go through each chapter thoroughly. Each one has its own vitally important message for you. So with this in mind, let's begin by seeing how people can strike out when playing the job hunt game, even when they have excellent qualifications.

1

MARKETING YOUR STRENGTHS

Most people misrepresent themselves when they are job hunting. Here are my dictionary's definitions of the word misrepresentation: "give the wrong impression of;" "calling attention to the wrong things;" "describe or portray wrongly."

These definitions are good for you to know because they give you a better understanding of how job hunters complicate their chances of getting meaningful employment. They send out their resumes for jobs that they know they can do — jobs that they have the necessary experience, skills, and abilities for, or jobs that they know they could easily learn if only given an opportunity — but strike out over and over again. This is mainly because their resumes are giving employers the wrong impression of their overall potential as an employee.

The bottom line is this. If you are hired to do a job instead of someone else, it is because you did a better job than the other person of selling the employer on your potential. In the employer's eyes, you look like a more promising employee so he or she is willing to gamble on you.

But, on the other hand, if you applied for a position you know you are qualified to do (or for a position that requires no previous work experience, just a willingness to learn) and didn't even get a job interview — despite the long hours of work you put into it — then you must be misrepresenting yourself. You must be calling the employer's attention to the wrong things about yourself.

This is quite disturbing when you think about it because it means that people with a lot to offer are being locked out of interesting career opportunities and tied to unrewarding jobs (or worse — the unemployment lines) all because they are misrepresenting themselves, mainly in writing on their resumes. They are not reaching the people who count (i.e., those with hiring power) in meaningful language; language that says: "I am loyal and hard-working, and capable of achieving excellent on-the-job results."

So do you have to have highly developed writing skills before you can sell yourself to an employer? Not at all. In fact, it is possible to persuade an employer that your knowledge and experience is more than adequate for a job opening without even knowing how to write a simple sentence. If you have any doubts about this, take a moment to browse through the resume samples at the end of this book. How often do you come across a complete sentence? You'll notice they very rarely appear. In fact, many of the sample resumes do not contain even one full sentence.

Then if it's not writing ability that wins employers over to your side, what is it that does? It is details. Details concerning your previously acquired knowledge and/or work experiences that say to an employer: "Here is what I did for my former employers. Give me an opportunity and I'll do the same and more for you." It is details that work for you; carefully selected details that persuade an employer he or she can expect to receive optimum returns on any investment made in you.

But instead of furnishing employers with important details on their background, job hunters (in general) try to convince themselves that details are not that terribly important. "If the employer is that deeply concerned with everything I've done," they can be heard saying, "then he can ask me about specific things during the job interview." However, this is the old famous last words talk. Unless you provide those important kinds of details to employers on your resume, you are never going to get that job interview.

What, then, are those details that employers want to see? Well, that is what this whole book is about. There are many vitally important details that job hunters fail to provide employers with (all of which will be dealt with thoroughly). However, for the time being, let's take a look at the most serious mistake job hunters make, and see what can be done to correct it.

The most serious mistake of all that most job hunters make (where they "call attention to the wrong things," "give the wrong impression of," "describe or portray wrongly") is in describing their duties and responsibilities for past employers. Most people do not have the slightest idea about what specific details they should highlight when accounting for their work experiences.

For example, a real estate agent, when describing his work experiences might feel comfortable with something like this:

> As a real estate agent with Housing Realty Limited in New York, NY, I was primarily responsible for selling residential, industrial and commercial properties.

And that might be all he states. Why? Because he takes it for granted, like many other people who have well-known job titles, that the prospective employer already knows what a real estate agent does; and if, by chance, he happens to be wrong about this, he assumes specific details can always be provided during the job interview.

But what if another real estate person, who described her duties in the following way, was in competition for a job against the real estate agent mentioned above. Whose background would look the most impressive? Which one do you think the employer would prefer to interview?

> Real Estate Agent for High House Realty Limited, in New York, NY.

Principal duties and responsibilities involved the following:

REAL ESTATE SALES: Responsible for selling residential, industrial and commercial properties; negotiating compromises and preparing legally binding agreements between buyers and sellers, under the Real Estate Act of New York; making property appraisals through both comparative and cost approaches; keeping informed and advising clients on market trends, business cycles, economic indicators, and trading strategies; promoting public awareness of the company through good client service;

MARKETING: Responsible for formulating sales strategy and direction (e.g., market development, major account sales activities, etc.); drafting and presenting proposals which emphasize the selling points and benefits of real estate handled by the company; creating and developing property promotional concepts/plans; assisting in the development of senior level policy and procedure;

FINANCING: Responsible for arranging financing for clients through trust companies, banks, credit and mortgage companies, as well as verifying the ability and determining the willingness of clients to pay (i.e., credit checks, personal interviews, etc.); approving mortgages.

The second account of the real estate agent's duties and responsibilities gives the employer something meaningful to deal with. It gives all kinds of important and interesting details that help the employer see more clearly what this applicant may be able to do. These details call attention to the "right" things and offer the employer encouraging reasons for assuming that this applicant is "loyal, hard-working, and capable of achieving excellent on-the-job results." Because of these details, the employer is apt to call this real estate agent and not the one we looked at first. The first real estate agent misrepresented himself.

Let's take one more example to further clarify how job hunters misrepresent themselves when describing their work experience. Unlike real estate agents (or those who think that employers know what they do by virtue of their job title), there are those who think that their job duties are so vast in scope and complicated in nature that it is impossible (and pointless) to even bother trying. A probation officer, for instance, would fit into this kind of category. One might describe previous probationary responsibilities this way:

> From September of 1990 to January of this year, I have been employed by the Ministry of Attorney General in Toronto, Ontario, as a probation officer. During this time, I have gained invaluable knowledge and experience in all aspects of probation work. I have enjoyed working with all my clients and have been instrumental in developing and implementing a wide range of adult and juvenile programs.

Now let's imagine that another probation officer (who had exactly the same type of responsibilities as the probation officer mentioned above) described his duties like this:

PROBATION OFFICER

Principal duties and responsibilities involved the following:

COUNSELING: Responsible for providing counseling services to adult criminal offenders, juvenile offenders, and the emotionally disturbed; discussing and resolving problems with clients, with respect and dignity shown at all times to those concerned, regardless of their type of offense or ethnic background; providing counseling services to clients who had experienced physical and sexual abuse, and/or problems associated with substance abuse, etc.;

CRISIS INTERVENTION: Responsible for providing on-the-scene emergency social intervention services to clients, when required; providing crisis intervention services on attempted suicides and for individuals experiencing severe emotional and/or psychiatric problems; making referrals for specialized assistance or treatment when necessary;

PROGRAM PLANNING: Responsible for providing guidance and advice on administrative problems and matters related to the implementation of various programs for adult criminal offenders (e.g., self-help, behavior modification, life skills, etc.); identifying and evaluating the need for new programs through consultation with appropriate institutional staff, clients, and public and private agencies; providing group training in the areas of self-esteem development and coping with peer pressure;

MAKING REFERRALS: Responsible for making referrals to appropriate government departments and social agencies (i.e., family court, Alcohol & Drug Commission, Forensic Psychiatric Clinic, police, lawyers, court staff, Ministry of Human Resources, Human Rights Branch, Ombudsman, Public Health, John Howard Society, and Public Employment Agencies, etc.).

The second analysis of the probation officer's responsibilities is obviously much more meaningful to read than the first one we looked at. There are only generalities in the first description, and these generalities,

along with the person who submitted them, will quickly be forgotten by the employer. The second analysis, however, is full of interesting facts — facts that will create a memorable impression in the mind of the reader.

So now you know the most serious mistake that job hunters make, and how it is best remedied. Your success in the job hunt is determined by how effective you are in marketing your work related strengths to employers. And to do this properly, you need a well-written resume.

2
RESUME OR CURRICULUM VITAE: A STRANGE NAME BUT A VALUABLE FRIEND

Do you know what a resume is? Or, more appropriately, do you know what advantages come to you personally from having a properly prepared resume?

To most people, the word "resume" conveys little meaning, if any meaning at all, to them. They may know that employers normally request job applicants to submit a copy of their resume to them, before being considered for a job opening; and that one purpose of having a resume is to condense one's educational background, work experience and personal information into a small, neat written form. But beyond these basic notions, only a small group of people (those who are presently enjoying the rewards of worthwhile jobs) know what a resume is and what it can do for them.

So let's begin by getting a clearer understanding of the word resume itself. Resume is French for "summary." Now when the word resume is applied to the job search it becomes a special kind of summary: a summary of your work related strengths.

Some people prefer to use the Latin expression *curriculum vitae* when referring to a summary of their work related strengths. The choice is personal. However, since the word resume is more commonly known, I will be using it throughout this book.

It is true that employers normally do request a resume from job applicants before deciding who to hire. And there is a simple explanation for this. They have to. They have to because you (as the job applicant) are the most valuable source of information that they can turn to for details about your background. This is an interesting observation, since who (out of all the people looking for work) is going to say anything damaging about him or herself on a resume? It is reasonable to assume that most people would be more inclined to proudly display their work related strengths and talents on their resume than they would be inclined to expose their weaknesses, shortcomings, and failings. So in light of this very natural proclivity of human nature, why do employers have to rely so heavily upon resumes before making their decision about who to hire in their firm?

This question is answered by asking another one: How else can an employer find out important details about a candidate's background except through the candidate? It's true that a prospective employer can call up your last five employers on the telephone to inquire about the type of worker you are. The prospective employer could also contact the people you provided as references and solicit anything they would like to volunteer about your character, general knowledge, verbal fluency and overall ability to organize your time and tasks.

But most employers are not likely to put themselves through all this; it's too time-consuming, perhaps expensive (e.g., long distance telephone calls), and in any case, not very likely to yield useful information. Former employers may be reluctant to provide the kind of enlightening remarks that could either help or hinder your chances.

Instead, the prospective employer is most willing to go by the statements you provide on your resume. And that's why you should take special care about what you say on it. The employer may be the final judge on who gets hired but you are the one who supplies the facts on which that decision rests.

A well-written resume serves many valuable purposes besides that of simply condensing your educational background, work experience, and personal information into a small and neat written form.

A properly prepared resume can also do the following for you:

(a) Get you a job interview
(b) Make the resumes submitted by those who are competing against you look weak and flimsy in their content in comparison to yours
(c) Greatly reduce the frustrations you normally encounter in the job search by providing more purposeful information on your background to employers, in a language they can easily relate to
(d) Help you clarify your most notable accomplishments and put your future career goals into a more meaningful perspective
(e) Strengthen your motivation and build up your morale for finding employment by giving you a more precise index of what is possible
(f) Help you critically review your past work experience in order to improve upon it in the future
(g) Permit you to immediately take advantage of career opportunities when they become available
(h) Help you to take control over your life rather than waiting around (perhaps forever) for the wheel of fortune to smile down upon you and spin you out a lucky break

For the employer, a well prepared resume on your background can do the following:

(a) Provide compelling reasons for granting you a job interview
(b) Tell more about the highlights of your background than a long or short conversation could ever reveal
(c) Clear up any lingering doubts about your ability to perform what is expected of you
(d) Point out that you have a sensitive awareness of the company's goals and needs
(e) Provide a strong indication of what your probable future contributions will be and your potential for advancement
(f) Help pin down your financial value to the company (i.e., your salary)
(g) Provide proof that you can communicate well in writing
(h) Provide valuable insights on the kind of person you are and the lifestyle you live
(i) Provide reasons for assuming that your personal needs would be well provided for if employed by the company (i.e., intellectual, creative, emotional, social, financial, etc.).

You can see from the above account of what a resume does for both you and the employer that it plays a very important role in the job search. It is a very valuable friend. So valuable in fact, that it can just about decide your fate in the job search. Because of this, you would think more people would spend more time preparing it. However, this is not what job hunters are doing.

What are job hunters doing instead of preparing a good resume?

They are relying upon standard application forms. What are these forms? Is there any advantage in filling them out? Can a standard application form etch the same image of your potential on an employer's mind as a well prepared resume? If not, then why do so many job applicants rely on them? Read the next chapter to find out the answers.

6

3

BASIC INGREDIENTS OF AN ORDINARY RESUME

Most job hunters do not have the faintest idea about what they should tell employers about themselves. And rather than troubling themselves to find out (unlike those of you who are reading this book) they tell themselves "details" are really not that important and that if the employer is really that interested in particulars he or she can quiz them during the job interview.

Perhaps it is this "I'll wait until I'm asked" attitude that explains why employers so often ask job applicants to fill in their standard application forms. They figure they had better have some questions of their own to ask job applicants, otherwise they may never find out what they need to know. Whatever the reason may be for the popularity of standard application forms, they are widely used and not, I might add, to anyone's advantage. Let's examine them for a moment.

The standard application form is used by the employer to collect job related information from candidates seeking employment with the company. It is, in a sense, similar to a resume in that it contains the three main categories of information that all resumes contain (i.e., personal information, educational background and work experience). However, unlike the resume, the standard application form does not permit applicants to provide details beyond these three categories. In fact, the applicant cannot even adequately discuss the questions asked within these areas.

Look, for example, at the standard application form in Sample #1 and compare the information collected on Laura T. Ladd to the information presented in her resume — see Resume #33 on page 141. Comparison shows how great an injustice is done to the job applicant. On the standard application form, this applicant must leave out any important details about herself that are not specifically asked for on the form. Not only this, but she is not allowed to elaborate on the chief responsibilities she had in any of her jobs for the simple reason there isn't sufficient room to elaborate.

In other words, Laura T. Ladd is misrepresenting herself on the standard application form. She is "giving the wrong impression" to the prospective employer of her potential. The one sure way of correcting this problem, however, would be by attaching a resume to the standard application form so that both would be reviewed together.

Another problem facing the job applicant when filling out standard application forms is this: you are writing down your answers from the top of your head and, as a result, may be inadvertently "calling attention to the wrong things." You need time to carefully think through these questions. For instance, stating what your duties and responsibilities were for former employers is impossible to do off the top of your head. To answer a question like that, you need to have either this book (i.e., the sample resumes to check) or an enormous amount of time to sift through exactly what you did. You cannot casually walk into a company from off the street and start writing up a detailed analysis of your background for the employer.

And then if your handwriting on this form is more like ancient hieroglyphics than anything legible, you are making matters even worse for yourself.

So what conclusion can we draw from our examination of the standard application form? This: never hand over a standard application form to an employer without also providing your resume. Why? Because if you do you will be misrepresenting yourself. You will be giving the employer very limited information about your work related strengths, and to make matters worse, you may be giving it in sloppy handwriting.

SAMPLE #1
STANDARD EMPLOYMENT APPLICATION FORM

STANDARD EMPLOYMENT APPLICATION FORM

PERSONAL INFORMATION

TYPE OF WORK APPLYING FOR: *Managerial*

STATE YOUR REASONS WHY: *Have extensive experience in this area.*

NAME: *Laura T. Ladd*

ADDRESS: *345 Personnel Lane*

CITY: *Olympia*

TELEPHONE NUMBER: *753-5555*

STATE/PROVINCE: *Washington*

ZIP/POSTAL CODE: *98504*

INDICATE ANY SPECIAL SKILLS AND ABILITIES YOU MAY HAVE: *Have strong negotiating skills and am a competent advocate in the field of labor law.*

ARE YOU LOOKING FOR FULL-TIME OR PART-TIME EMPLOYMENT? *full-time*

WHEN WILL YOU BE AVAILABLE FOR WORK? *Minimum one month's notice required*

HAVE YOU EVER BEEN EMPLOYED BY THIS COMPANY? *No*

EDUCATION RECORD

NAME, LOCATION OF INSTITUTION	COURSES TAKEN/MAJOR	CERTIFICATION EARNED (i.e., Diploma, TQ, etc.)	FROM/TO
SENIOR HIGH *West Central High School*		*Grade 12 Diploma*	*1967-1970*
VOCATIONAL/ BUSINESS			
UNIVERSITY/ COLLEGE	*Business Administration*	*Bachelor of Commerce*	*1970-1973*
POST GRADUATE			

SPECIAL COURSES TAKEN *Labor law, Local Administration and Assertiveness Legislative Procedures, General Labor Relations*

WORK EXPERIENCE

NAME OF EMPLOYER _City Center Hospital_

DUTIES _(Please refer to attached resume)_ _____

_____

LOCATION_____

POSITION/JOB TITLE _Director of Personnel_ DATES OF EMPLOYMENT _August 1973 – present_

SUPERVISOR _Mr. Mel Sharp_ _____

REASON FOR LEAVING _Desire a position that provides more opportunities_

for professional growth and continual self-development. _____

FULL-TIME ___✓_____ PART-TIME_____

NAME OF EMPLOYER_____

DUTIES _____

****

LOCATION_____

POSITION/JOB TITLE_____ DATES OF EMPLOYMENT_____

SUPERVISOR_____

REASON FOR LEAVING_____

FULL-TIME_____ PART-TIME_____

NAME OF EMPLOYER_____

DUTIES _____

****

LOCATION_____

POSITION/JOB TITLE_____ DATES OF EMPLOYMENT_____

SUPERVISOR_____

REASON FOR LEAVING_____

FULL-TIME_____ PART-TIME_____

4
BEYOND THE MERE ESSENTIALS: RESUMES THAT REDUCE THE EMPLOYER'S GUESS WORK

If there was no such thing as competition for employment, you would not need a resume. For, without competition, there would be no need to prove to employers that you are the best person for the job. Instead, you would only have to provide them with the mere essentials about yourself, and that basic requirement could easily be met by filling in a standard application form.

Unfortunately (or fortunately, depending on how competitive you may be), competition for employment does exist. Employers are accustomed to receiving all kinds of applications for their job openings; and because of this they will obviously hire the one candidate who promises to offer them the most for their money.

And how do employers decide who the most promising candidate is? They do this by addressing themselves to one very important question: "Which candidate (out of all those who have the basic qualifications for the job) has offered the most to past employers?" Whoever this candidate is will be the one chosen.

The most reliable means employers have of predicting how successful an employee you will be is this: your past work record. If you have worked well for other employers, then the chances are excellent you will work just as well in the future. Thus, by simply examining your work record, prospective employers can get a reasonably good indication of how strong your contributions will be to their company.

But where do employers get this "work record" of you? They get it from you when you give them your resume.

"Fine," you say. "But what kind of information are employers looking for on my resume to predict the type of contributions that I'll make?"

Employers will look for any information you include on your resume that has a significant bearing on the kind of position you are applying for. Examples of this kind of information might include the following:

Educational Background

Vocational/business training

Degrees or credits earned

Courses studied

Honors and scholarships

Work Experience

Past employers

Job classification at start and end

Chief responsibilities

Special projects and assignments

Supervisory responsibilities and extent to which you worked independently

Reasons for leaving past employers and explanations for gaps in employment

Military Experience

Duration of enlistment

Assigned rank at start and end

Chief responsibilities

Special recognitions and achievements

Type of discharge

Adequacy of career choice

Pride in work

Degree of personal interest in work

Internally or externally committed to work (i.e., here for the money or here because you like the work itself)

Professional interests

Job related knowledge

Depth of knowledge relating to job and ability to define specific tasks

Company sponsored courses, workshops and seminars attended

Quality and speed of decisions

Ability to make good judgments independently

Resilience in stressful situations

Thoroughness and accuracy in the completion of tasks

Originality of ideas

Openness to new perspectives

Capacity to undergo further on-the-job training

Competency in carrying out instructions

Depth of understanding of company's goals and long-range objectives

Ability to identify and assess good business opportunities

Perceptiveness in observing strains and stresses of clients and fellow workers

Objectivity

Emotional Stability

Capacity to effectively handle customer complaints

Willingness to take a team approach to problem solving

Coolness in the face of unusual pressures

Ability to handle criticisms from fellow workers/supervisors, etc.

Motivation

Personal desire for challenging duties and responsibilities

Personal long-range expectations with the company

Constructive activities engaged in during leisure hours

Ability to organize own personal time and tasks efficiently

Ability to work with enthusiasm and high energy on all assignments

Supervisory or leadership skills

Ability to project an excellent company image to clients and subordinates

Willingness to make personal sacrifices in fulfilling company goals

Special skills and abilities

Ability to promote cooperation among workers

Skill in organizing and implementing special projects

Ability to interpret and implement top policy and procedure

Ability to clarify company objectives in writing and orally

Strength of interpersonal communication skills

Ability to establish and promote high performance standards

Knowledge of safety standards and equipment

Ability to analyze and achieve key results for company

Organizing, managing, and motivating skills

Potential

Capacity for professional growth and self-development

Willingness to relocate to another company branch

Ranking of knowledge and experience against others in the same job classification

For the time being do not concern yourself with "how" to provide employers with information on these areas. That will become clear to you after reading chapter 6 on "Instructions."

The most important point to keep in mind here is that employers want to have their curiosity about you (in the above areas) satisfied. They want you to supply them with evidence — especially evidence from past on-the-job experiences — of what you have to offer them in: education, work experience, motivation, potential, etc. The stronger the evidence that you can give prospective employers in these areas, the more likely they are to feel favorably disposed toward you.

In those fields of employment where competition is the stiffest, your resume must contain more than the mere essentials if you hope to make the shortlist (i.e., the list of names an employer has of applicants to be interviewed). You must be able to persuade the employer that your potential contributions to the company justify hiring you.

5

COMMON MISTAKES: WHAT TO WATCH OUT FOR
BEFORE PREPARING YOUR RESUME

a. WRITING TOO MUCH

The number of pages in your resume will mainly be determined by the total number of jobs you have had and how relevant each one is to the kind of position you are applying for. When deciding whether or not your resume is too long, use the samples provided in this book as a guideline, and then ask yourself this question. Do all the details defining my duties and responsibilities have a significant bearing on the kind of position I am applying for? If your answer is "yes," then your resume is not too long; however, if your answer is "a lot of my details are not relevant to the job I'm applying for," then your resume is too long and needs to be shortened, without showing any mercy to the unnecessary parts.

b. BEING TOO WORDY

Which of the following two statements do you think is most effective?

(a) I was considered an able organizer of committee meetings and had many compliments from my superiors on how well I maintained the records of expenditure.

(b) Duties included organizing committee meetings as well as maintaining records of expenditure.

There are half as many words in the second statement as in the first; yet the second statement is more telling and less tedious to read.

The prospective employer has a lot of resumes to read besides yours. Give your best points in brief and precise language.

c. ARRANGING JOB RESPONSIBILITIES IN ANY OLD ORDER

Your job duties and responsibilities should be arranged in order of importance. You do this so the employer can see right away what major duties you may have had without having to search for them.

d. USING THE WORD "I" TOO OFTEN

When you write a resume, it is very easy to fall into the habit of using the first person pronoun "I." For instance, saying "I supervised eight employees; I hired and trained all personnel; I directed and assisted in the investigations of accidents; I recommended appropriate corrective or disciplinary action; I promoted constructive thinking among all staff members, etc."

Makes you sound as though you are in love with yourself, doesn't it?

To get around this problem of sounding self-centered, all you need to do is use an "-ing" form of verb at the beginning of each point you wish to make. The above example corrected would look like this: "supervising eight employees; hiring and training of all personnel; directing and assisting in the investigation of accidents; recommending appropriate corrective or disciplinary action; promoting constructive thinking among all staff members, etc."

e. USING TOO MUCH TECHNICAL JARGON

Technical jargon is okay to use if the person reading your resume is already familiar with your terms of reference. Otherwise, your resume will look like a foreign language to whoever ends up reviewing it. For example, let's say an intermediate environmental technician (even the job title sounds jargonish) stated these responsibilities on her resume: measuring gas stream particulate concentrations from stationary sources; collecting and monitoring air emission samples from prescribed areas; determining the salt content from particulate concentrations; analyzing samples of water for pH measurements, total dissolved solids, total suspended solids, alkalinity, dustfall, chlorides, turbidity, etc.

All the above duties accurately and succinctly describe an intermediate environmental technician's job; however, who (except an environmental technician and associates) would be able to understand the terminology used?

To the average person this would make much more sense: intermediate environmental technician — primarily responsible for air, water and waste-water analysis.

So unless you can see a justifiable reason for using technical talk, avoid it.

f. MAKING ERRORS IN SPELLING, GRAMMAR, AND PUNCTUATION

Double check your spelling, grammar and punctuation. By doing so, you will be that much more effective in convincing the prospective employer that you are a neat and accurate person. **Note:** If you are a Canadian citizen applying to a Canadian company, use Canadian spelling.

Try to keep most words spelled out in full. Sometimes, however, this is not al-ways possible to do or necessarily appropriate (for example, your middle initial (you could, of course, spell your whole name out in full, it's up to you); or (for those who were aboard military vessels) names of ships like H.M.C.S. Provider).

g. SUBMITTING A HAND-WRITTEN RESUME

Sometimes jobs advertised in the newspaper will ask you to reply in your own handwriting. This type of request will indicate to you that good handwriting is an essential requirement of the job, or that the employer is using handwriting analysis to screen applicants. You can satisfy this request by submitting a handwritten copy of your letter of introduction. There is no need for handwriting your whole resume.

h. DRAWING ATTENTION TO YOUR MOONLIGHTING ACTIVITIES

Don't draw attention to any part-time jobs you may have had while working full-time. To many employers, evidence of moonlighting on your resume might suggest to them that you tend to overextend yourself, and therefore may occasionally be coming in to work too tired to do what is expected of you.

i. MENTIONING YOUR BELIEFS

You probably would not write on your resume, "I'm a member of the XYZ political party," but you might imply it by saying you did volunteer work for them.

You probably would not say on your resume that you belong to ABC religious denomination, but you could impart that message by indicating you do ABC religious activities. Be cautious about this, as it could prejudice your application. However, if most of your experience has been in volunteer work, you will have to include it. In that case, emphasize the nature of your work and responsibilities rather than the organization for which you worked.

j. STRESSING YOUR NEEDS AND NOT THE EMPLOYERS'

There is sometimes a great temptation to discuss what you want and need on a resume. However, your principal objective at all times is to convince employers that you and only you are who they are looking for.

To do this, you must at all times stress their needs on your resume by showing how your knowledge and experience can be used to fulfill them.

k. CONTRADICTING YOURSELF

It is very easy to contradict yourself when writing a resume. So easy in fact that sometimes an honest mistake can make you look like a colossal liar. Mistake or not, it's all the same to prospective employers. Therefore, be especially cautious in your use of dates — that's where most contradictions occur.

l. EXAGGERATING

Whenever you feel the urge to paint a sensational account of your past on-the-job accomplishments, do your best to resist it. Your special accomplishments are of interest to the prospective employer and very definitely should be mentioned, but in a moderate way.

m. MENTIONING RELATIVES AND THEIR OCCUPATIONS

There is absolutely no advantage in calling attention to what your father and mother do (or did) for a living or your son(s) or daughter(s) (i.e., John attends law school at the University of Texas and has one lovely daughter). Do these details have any bearing on your qualifications or ability to perform the job? Your father, mother, daughters, sons and everyone else in your family tree may all be terrific people. However, when you apply for employment with a particular firm, you will be judged on your own merits.

n. SAYING YOUR FRIENDS CONSIDER YOU "ATTRACTIVE" OR "WELL GROOMED"

If physical attributes and overall appearances are vital considerations for the type of work you seek, then put a color picture (passport picture size) in with your resume. It will be a more reliable guide to your beauty than the subjective opinions of your friends. Besides, for all the employer may know, those same people who are saying that you are "attractive" and "well groomed" may also think that sneakers and jogging shorts are perfect apparel for most types of job interviews.

o. USING HUMOR

You are taking an unnecessary risk when you toss in a line or two of humor either in your resume or your covering letter. It is a business proposition that you are offering to a business person — (i.e., your services in exchange for their wages).

p. STATING YOUR HEALTH AS FAIR

If your health is not excellent or good, then just do not make any reference to this area. Saying that your health is fair is like making a voluntary admission that you have serious health problems.

q. USING AN INAPPROPRIATE ITEM HEADING FOR YOUR WORK EXPERIENCE

You should stress the nature of your work experience — if you intend to stay in your field — by choosing an item heading that is compatible with it. For instance, if all your work experience has been in teaching then use the item heading "TEACHING EXPERIENCE" when you begin accounting for past employers.

Likewise, if you were a doctor, lawyer or any type of professional person, take advantage of an item heading like "PROFESSIONAL EXPERIENCE."

Other examples of item headings that you might like to choose from are: "MILITARY EXPERIENCE," "BUSINESS EXPERIENCE," "EMPLOYMENT SUMMARY," "EMPLOYMENT HISTORY," "WORK BACKGROUND," "WORK EXPERIENCE."

Now you should have a pretty good idea of what not to do when preparing your own resume. The next chapter tells you what you need to do when aiming for professional results on your resume.

But first, look at the resume in Sample #2. It is a good example of how to give the wrong impression of your work related strengths to an employer.

It is an example of a medical secretary's resume, but it could have been anyone's, including yours or mine.

This example of a poorly constructed resume provides only vague generalities about the person it represents (or rather misrepresents). And vague generalities are not what is needed to create a lasting impression in the mind of the reader.

So take the necessary time to study the following resume. After you collect a good sense of its deficiencies, turn to Sample #3 and study the corrected version. Now compare and contrast the two samples. Which one would you prefer to have representing you?

SAMPLE #2
POORLY CONSTRUCTED RESUME

Joyce C. Scribe

<u>EDUCATION</u>

1974   Iowa Community College, Stenographic Program

1973   Graduate, Des Moines High School, College Prep

<u>WORK EXPERIENCE</u>

1980 - present Des Moines Medical Clinic. Job title: Medical Secretary. I am involved in all activities pertaining to secretarial functions, including general office duties, typing and filing. I have the sole responsibility for the maintenance of records, correspondence, resource materials, and office supplies. I am very effective in dealing with all patients, and handle all travel arrangements for the doctors.

1973 - 1980   Dr. George Helper (General Practitioner). Job title: Medical Secretary. My responsibilities in this job were very much the same as what I did for the Des Moines Medical Clinic.

<u>INTERESTS</u>

enjoy knitting, sewing, tie dying, and handpainting on silk

<u>SKILLS</u>

I have some knowledge of word processing and computerized accounting programs, and take pride in my communication skills

<u>PERSONAL</u>

23 Main Street
Des Moines, IA 51319
Phone: (515) 281-2222

<u>REFERENCES</u>   Dr. Ralph Sharp, (515) 281-3333
Dr. George Helper, (515) 281-4444

Joyce C. Scribe
23 Main Street
Des Moines, IA 51319

Home telephone: (515) 281-2222

PERSONAL INFORMATION

Birth date: January 1, 1954
Health: excellent

EDUCATIONAL BACKGROUND

Stenographic Program: Iowa Community College, Des Moines, Iowa, 1974

Diploma (Grade 12 Academic): Des Moines High School, Des Moines, Iowa, 1973

SPECIAL SKILLS AND ABILITIES

- Possess strong interpersonal communication skills, and have a demonstrated interest in working harmoniously with others
- Can present a professional image to patients, fellow workers, subordinates and/or peers

KNOWLEDGE OF COMPUTER APPLICATIONS

WordPerfect (5.1); Lotus 1-2-3; Bedford Accounting; Word Processing

HOBBIES AND INTERESTS: meeting people; reading literature; physical fitness

AVAILABILITY: Minimum of two weeks' notice required.

SALARY EXPECTED: Open — nature and challenge of position itself is of principal concern.

PROFESSIONAL EXPERIENCE

July 1980 – present: full-time employment
        Des Moines Medical Clinic
        123 Hospital Street
        Des Moines, Iowa

Medical Secretary for this 4-Doctor Medical Clinic. Reporting directly to
        the Senior Doctor on objectives and results, principal duties and
        responsibilities involve the following:

PUBLIC RELATIONS: Responsible for answering in a polite and profesio
        nal manner the inquiries and/or complaints of patients; confirming
        the appointments of outside callers, as well as receiving and directing
        such persons to the appropriate Doctors; promoting public awareness of
        the clinic through the provision of good care and service to patients;

SCHEDULING PATIENTS: Responsible for making the necessary arrangements for
        the booking of patients with appropriate Doctors and Health Care
        Professionals and/or for surgical intervention; booking out-patient
        procedures and in-patient procedures, as well as all X-rays, Scans,
        and Lab Work; preparing and/or processing Medicare Forms, Insurance
        Forms, Workers' Compensation Forms, and Disability Forms;

SAMPLE #3 — Continued

OFFICE ADMINISTRATION: Responsible for maintaining a calendar of appointments and meetings for the Doctors; typing and composing of letters
and memos for signature, with the responsibility for their correct
grammar, spelling and punctuation; transcribing and typing minutes of
conferences and meetings, memos, reports, statements, etc. from
written notes or verbal instructions; maintaining confidential filing
systems; setting up travel arrangements for the Doctors when they
planned to attend out-of-town medical conferences, business meetings
and conventions (e.g., contacting travel agencies; booking airfares
and hotel accommodations; arranging itineraries).

June 1973 - July 1980: full-time employment
Dr. George Helper, General Practitioner
4321 1st Avenue
Des Moines, Iowa

Medical Secretary: Principal duties and responsibilities were similar in
nature to those discussed above.

BUSINESS REFERENCES

Dr. Ralph Sharp, General Practitioner
Des Moines Medical Clinic
123 Hospital Street
Des Moines, Iowa
Office telephone: (515) 281-3333

Dr. George Helper, General Practitioner
4321 1st Avenue
Des Moines, Iowa
Office telephone: (515) 281-4444

6

INSTRUCTIONS: HOW TO
PROFESSIONALLY PREPARE YOUR RESUME

What reasons can you give to a prospective employer to persuade him or her to grant you a job interview? This is the question that your resume needs to answer in concise, forceful, and easy-to-understand terms, each time you apply for a job.

In this chapter you will be shown a variety of steps on how to prepare your resume. Each one of these steps, when it is relevant to the position you are applying for, provides a prospective employer with one particular reason why he or she should grant you a job interview.

Thus, to ensure you are using the steps in this chapter to your best advantage, all you have to do is carefully consider how relevant each and every one is to the job you are applying for. Those steps that are relevant to the job you are applying for should be copied word-for-word into your resume; and those steps that are not relevant need to be kept out, as their presence in your resume will only serve to make it longer than it needs to be.

To clearly illustrate how to use the steps in this chapter effectively, let's say, for example, you had over five years management experience in a grocery store and a grade 12 diploma, and wanted to apply for the following job, which you saw advertised in your local newspaper (see Sample #4).

The underlined parts of this advertisement tell you the principal requirements of this job. Thus, of all the steps included in this chapter, Steps 5 (Educational Background), Step 15 (Travel), Step 23 (Special Training) and Step 27 (Work Experience) are the ones most relevant to the requirements of this position. We know this because the advertisement itself makes direct references to them. Consequently, using these steps on your resume would give this prospective employer your best reasons for being granted a job interview. Read through Steps 5, 15, 23, and 27, and then turn to sample Resume #24: Grocery Store Manager on page 126 to see how these (and other helpful steps) have been used to advantage in this resume.

Obviously not everyone reading this book would need to use the above mentioned steps in their resume, for not everyone is hoping to find work as a grocery store manager. Some readers may be systems analysts, others may be nurses; some may be corporate executives, others may be psychologists; some may be students, others may be teachers, and so forth. Consequently, different steps will apply to different backgrounds.

In deciding which particular steps in this chapter are most relevant to the position you are applying for, study the examples of good resumes for various jobs in the Appendix of this book. They will show you how people in positions similar to yours have capitalized on their assets in their resumes.

Use the worksheets following the instructions for your draft copy. They have been included for your convenience. You may find that a pencil rather than a pen will be more helpful for filling in the blanks (in case you need to erase any mistakes).

SAMPLE #4
JOB ADVERTISEMENT

Grocery Store Supervisor

This position requires <u>ongoing travel</u> to our grocery store locations throughout California. You will be responsible for the operational management of three of our stores, employing over 120 staff.

Your responsibilities will include <u>staff supervision, customer relations, creating and developing promotional concepts</u> in your assigned stores, <u>and general office administrative duties</u>.

Qualified candidates will have their <u>grade 12 diploma</u> and a minimum of <u>five years retail management experience in a progressive grocery store</u>.

Remuneration is competitive and includes a company vehicle, a complete benefit package, and <u>opportunity for advancement</u>.

Candidates must demonstrate through their resume how they meet the requirements of this position. All resumes should be sent to: Human Resources Department, Sunrise Groceries Ltd., P.O. Box 32, Sacramento, California 91234.

The following steps are keyed to the numbers in Worksheet #1, Resume Worksheet, on page 29.

STEP 1: NAME

First of all write your complete name in the space you see provided on the worksheet. Your middle name can be spelled out in full or represented by an initial.

What if the name you go by in your social life is not the one you go by in your business life? In this type of situation you would enter your real name first and then have it followed (in brackets) by your other name. For example: your real name may be Janet R. Scott but among friends you might be called Jan. Thus you would enter your name as Janet (Jan) R. Scott.

STEP 2: ADDRESS

Ideally your home or resident address should be used as your mailing address. Sometimes, however, you may find yourself having to use a "c/o" or "General Delivery" on your resume. But, in doing so you will look unsettled in the community to the prospective employer. So ask a friend if you can use his or her address for your mail until you find a permanent place to hang your hat; also ask if you can leave out the "c/o."

STEP 3: TELEPHONE

Your home telephone should be entered first; telephone numbers for your office, messages, or fax would follow. Remember to include area codes.

STEP 4: PERSONAL INFORMATION

In the United States, the Civil Rights Act, which became law in 1964, prohibits discrimination in employment practices on the basis of race, color, religion, sex, or national origin. And akin to this legislation in Canada is the Canadian Human Rights Act, which prohibits an employer from refusing to hire a job applicant because of his or her race, national or ethnic origin, color, religion, age, sex, marital status, family status, disability, or conviction for which a pardon has been granted.

That's the law. But there is nothing stipulated in the law that says an employer must give a job interview to a job applicant. Thus, an employer who thinks you are in bad health, overweight and too old or too young for the job opening does not have to grant you an interview.

So use your own good discretion here. The sample resumes in this book will give you an idea as to what you can call attention to under this section, should you decide to.

STEP 5: EDUCATIONAL BACKGROUND

What was the last educational program that you were enrolled in? That would be the one you enter first on your resume. Were there any special courses or areas of concentration within this program that you worked on? If so, consider mentioning them if they relate to whatever type of work you are applying for. What is the name of the institution you attended when taking this program? What city, state/province is it located in? In what year did you complete this program?

These are the kind of questions you must answer for each program you were enrolled in. However, there is no need to go back any further than your grade 12 diploma.

What if you were in a program that you did not complete? In this case, you would say "successfully completed *(enter a number here)* years of this *(enter a number here)* year program" just after mentioning the state/province where the college or university is located.

What about mentioning special honors and/or scholarships you may have received? Here you must use your own discretion. Just ask yourself this: if I mention receiving any honors or scholarships will I look like a person with too much potential for this job? If your answer is "yes," then you know what to do.

But if your answer is "no," then state the name of your award, the amount of money you received, the period it covered and the reason you won it.

STEP 6: SPECIAL COURSES TAKEN

List any courses you may have taken that were not part of a regular educational program. These could be courses that were sponsored by companies you worked for or courses you paid for yourself.

By putting this kind of information on your resume you are saying two things to an employer: you have continued to find challenges for your mind since leaving school, and you have acquired significant theoretical knowledge that relates directly to the position you are applying for.

Enter your special courses on the resume beginning with the last one you took (i.e., reverse chronological order). State the name of the course, where you studied it (i.e., institution, city, state/province, and the year you completed it).

STEP 7: WORKSHOPS AND SEMINARS

One way of getting across the idea to an employer that you really like your work is to mention the work related workshops and seminars you attended. No one is forced into attending a workshop or seminar. You go only because you are genuinely interested in your career. So provide the employer with this kind of information by stating what the workshop was called, where it was held (i.e., institution, city, state/province) and who sponsored it.

STEP 8: VOLUNTEER WORK EXPERIENCE

How are your social skills? Can you take a team approach to problem solving or must things be done according to your rules all the time?

You can imply you work cooperatively with others and/or that you are also community-minded by listing organizations that you have done volunteer work for.

If your duties, while serving in a volunteer capacity, have much in common with the job you are applying for, this would be another good reason for mentioning your volunteer work. For example, if you are a social worker, you may have volunteered some of your time to a telephone crisis line;

or if you are a special education teacher, you may have helped people with learning difficulties in your spare time. In other words, include any volunteer work that helps demonstrate you have an ongoing interest in your particular field of employment.

However, be on guard! Try not to mention activities that give away your religious or political leanings. For instance, if you state that you are a member of The True Believers Church board and held the office of deacon for three years, and the person reviewing your resume is a headstrong atheist, where do you think your resume will end up?

Therefore play it safe. You do not have a clue about the person assessing your background; there is not much sense in losing a good job opportunity just because your personal beliefs happen to be different from the prospective employer's.

Set up your volunteer work experience by indicating the name of the organization you donated your time to, its street address and location (i.e., city, state/province). Give yourself a title (even if you were not officially given one), and then briefly describe your contributions. Indicate the length of time you were involved with this organization; and, if it is not well known, describe in a line or two the kind of services it provides in the community.

STEP 9: SPECIAL LICENSES AND/OR CERTIFICATES

With all else being equal, you could get the edge over another job applicant simply because you possess a special license or certificate. Suppose, for example, that you applied for work in a bank as a Teller. There would be lots of competition for the job, right? But you are a Teller who has an emergency first aid certificate, and for this reason you are a more valuable asset to the bank. Why? Because you are safety oriented. You would know what to do if someone got hurt on the job or if a customer

experienced a health-related problem while visiting the bank. Thus you are serving the interest of the prospective employer (not to mention the customer!) in a very special way.

In setting up this type of information on your resume, enter the name of the certificate or license first, followed by the name of the institution that conferred it upon you, its location, and finally, the date you received it.

STEP 10: PROFESSIONAL AFFILIATIONS/SOCIETIES

If you have professional work experience, then mention any professional affiliations or societies you hold (or held) membership in.

STEP 11: UNION MEMBERSHIPS

Only mention membership in a union when it is relevant to the kind of position you are applying for.

STEP 12: PATENTS/PUBLICATIONS

If you have any publications that your prospective employer should know about, refer to Resume #39: Psychologist on page 153 for an example on how to include them.

When citing any patents you may have, be sure to include the patent number.

STEP 13: SPECIAL SKILLS AND ABILITIES

Read over the statements on special skills and abilities that are found in the sample resumes. Consider including those which are relevant to the type of position you are seeking.

STEP 14: KNOWLEDGE OF LANGUAGES

Sometimes knowing a second language can be an advantage when looking for certain kinds of work (i.e., public relations person, tour guide, flight attendant). If you see an advantage in entering your ability to communicate in another language, give your reading, writing, speaking and comprehension ability as good, fair, or excellent.

STEP 15: TRAVEL

Some positions, like sales representatives, truck drivers, and flight attendants, require various degrees of travelling. If the position you are applying for requires you to travel, frequently or infrequently, then say you are willing to comply with all travelling requirements.

STEP 16: RELOCATE

There may not be an immediate job opening at the business where you are seeking employment. But perhaps one of its branch offices has an opening. In this situation, would you consider relocating?

Maybe the type of work you are seeking requires a willingness to relocate occasionally. If so, say you are willing to relocate on your resume.

STEP 17: AVAILABILITY

If you are presently unemployed and do not have any business or personal obligations, say you are available immediately.

But if you are employed, you will need to give your current employer reasonable notice of your intention to leave. You will be only hurting yourself if you don't. Why? Because the chances are that you have mentioned the fact that you are employed on your resume. The prospective employer who reads this will wonder why you are not giving sufficient notice to your present employer. Would you also leave your new job on short notice?

Give the normal two to four weeks notice if you are already employed.

STEP 18: PRESENT EMPLOYER

Is it all right for the prospective employer to contact your present employer without jeopardizing your job? If yes, then say this on your resume: "My present employer is prepared to discuss any questions regarding my work record at this time. (Please refer to the Business References provided at the end of this resume for the name, address, and business telephone of the individual to contact)."

On the other hand, if you have not yet informed your boss of your decision to leave, say this: "My present employer is currently unaware of my decision to seek other employment; however, he/she may be contacted to answer any questions about my work record, after first notifying myself of your intention to do so." By this last statement on your resume, you are letting the prospective employer know that you are not being dismissed (you are still on good terms with your employer).

STEP 19: BONDABLE

Everyone is bondable. Yes, even the person who has a criminal record is bondable.

All it takes to be bonded is an insurance company that agrees to reimburse an employer for any losses experienced while you are employed there. Of course, the insurance company that is issuing the bond is supposed to conduct a background check to determine whether or not you do in fact have a criminal record, bad credit rating, poor employment record, etc. But the decision on whether to bond you lies with the insurance company itself. If you had all these black marks against you, the insurance company may be reluctant to issue a bond but they could if they wanted to.

People working in a place where they have easy access to cash and/or valuables may have to be bonded.

STEP 20: SHIFTWORK

By agreeing to work shiftwork, you will come across more favorably to an employer since not many people like working irregular hours. Of course, if the job you are applying for only involves working during regular business hours, there is no point in stating you would agree to working shiftwork on your resume.

STEP 21: RESERVE DUTY

Reserve duty means being on call 24 hours per day — not a very pleasant thought for many people. Sometimes, however, it's necessary for certain kinds of employment (e.g., flight attendants).

One advantage in stating your willingness to work reserve duty is that you will appear very interested in the kind of work you seek. Only a person who is genuinely interested in a particular job would hang around a telephone 24 hours per day waiting to be called in.

STEP 22: OVERTIME

If you are prepared to put in extra hours of work for your employer, be sure to mention this on your resume. By saying this you will appear dedicated to your employer.

STEP 23: SPECIAL TRAINING

Would you like to advance within the ranks of the company you are eventually employed by? Would you at least like to give this impression? By agreeing to undergo further training (either on-the-job or off-the-job) you are suggesting to the employer that you are trainable, adaptable, and capable of growth within the company.

Of course, if you already know there never will be any opportunity for advancement within the ranks of the company you hope to be employed by, there is no point in mentioning this on you resume.

STEP 24: PROFESSIONAL INTERESTS

Think of something work related that you enjoy doing during your leisure hours that is similar to what you do during your working hours. For example, a Systems Analyst might say his or her professional interest is: keeping abreast of the ongoing changes, trends, and developments in state-of-the-art computer hardware and software. As you look through the sample resumes in the appendix, you will see plenty of examples of how people with professional backgrounds have made this step work for them.

STEP 25: HOBBIES AND INTERESTS

There are three principal reasons for mentioning hobbies and interests on your resume. First, your hobbies and interests can be used to suggest that you have good social skills (by saying you like meeting people or by mentioning various group activities you participate in); second, if the job you are seeking is more taxing mentally than physically, you can suggest that you enjoy intellectual pursuits (by saying, for example, that you enjoy reading literature); and third, you can suggest that you are in good physical condition (by mentioning certain sports or physically demanding activities that you enjoy participating in).

Look over the examples of hobbies and interests found in the sample resumes for ideas on what you can say.

STEP 26: SALARY EXPECTED

There are three main reasons why you may want to discuss your salary expectations on a resume. First, you may have to. The job you are applying for (if advertised in the newspaper) may request that all candidates are to state their salary expectations.

Second, you may want to indicate to the prospective employer that it is the job you are most interested in and not the money. (Good for the career-minded person).

Third, you may want to say the opposite to the above: that it is the money you are most interested in, not so much the work itself. (Good for high-powered sales people.)

Whatever your main concern is, never pin yourself down to a precise figure. In saying exactly what you want in salary you might hurt your chances of being granted a job interview. Why? Because your figure could be higher or lower than what the employer intends to pay.

Thus, if it's the job that you are most interested in and not the salary, say this:

"Open — nature and challenge of position itself is of principal concern."

On the other hand, if it's the money that is most important to you, say: "Negotiable."

Both of the above statements on salary diplomatically handle this somewhat controversial subject.

STEP 27: WORK EXPERIENCE

When defining your duties and responsibilities for any given position you may have had, you will need to rely heavily upon the job descriptions given in the sample resumes.

The first job you enter on the worksheet is the one you are either employed in now or the one you last had. The next job would be the next most recent one and so forth. In other words, arrange your jobs in reverse chronological order beginning with the most recent one.

Keep in mind that you do not have to account for every job you have had. A day's work (or a couple of weeks) here and there is too insignificant to mention.

Starting with the most recent job you had (or have), enter your dates of employment (including the months). Remember that the more details you have, the more credibility you have.

To the right of your employment dates for each job, state whether your various jobs were full-time, part-time, term, temporary, summer employment or auxiliary positions.

Then give the name of the business with its street address, city, state/province.

Next, give yourself a job title. If you did not have one officially bestowed upon you then make one up. For example, if you were helping out in a wide number of ways and not spending your time mainly engaged in one particular area, call yourself a resource person.

Alongside of your job title, you may want to include a line or two that defines the nature of the services or products provided by the company you worked for. In other words, their reason for being in existence. (You will see lots of examples of how to define a company in the sample resumes).

What if the job title you had upon leaving was not the title you had when you started? You were promoted, in other words. Use the following example as a guide for entering any promotions you may have had:

> Promoted from the position of Sales Representative (October 1978 – December 1979) to Division Manager (December 1979 – February 1980) to Regional Manager (February 1980 – October 1984) to Assistant to the Vice President (October 1984 – April 1988) to the position of Vice President (April 1988 – present)

After entering your job title (as well as any promotions you may have had) and defining the company you worked for, proceed to describe your duties and responsibilities. Do so by finding duties in the sample resumes that are similar to what you have done.

Those responsibilities that are like what you have done but not exactly the same just need to be modified to suit your particular situation.

Notice in the sample resumes (see Appendix) how jobs involving various levels of responsibility are described. For example, in Resume #6 on page 99, we can see at a glance that the person represented by this resume had three key areas of responsibility while employed as a Bookkeeper. These key responsibilities consisted of general accounting, bookkeeping, and managing payroll procedures. Each of these three key areas of responsibility can be easily identified by a prospective employer on this resume because they have all been typed in bold capital letters to make them stand out on the page. This is a feature that's available on a word processor, and on typewriters by striking each letter twice. Another way to make key areas and titles stand out is to underline them (see Resume #15 on page 112).

Then, alongside of each of these various levels of responsibility (i.e., general accounting, bookkeeping, and managing payroll procedures), supporting details are provided to spell out the specific nature of contributions made in these areas.

You too should follow this type of approach when describing your various positions. In highlighting key responsibilities in this way, you are helping the prospective employer read through your resume quickly, without the risk of anything important being overlooked.

Remember to arrange your duties and responsibilities in order of importance, so the prospective employer can see at a glance what your principal responsibilities were.

STEP 28: REASON FOR LEAVING

When deciding whether or not to include a reason for leaving, just ask yourself this question: Am I raising more questions than I'm answering by including my reason for leaving? If your answer is yes, then don't bother putting one in. However, be sure you have some reasonable explanation ready in case you are asked for one during the job interview.

Here are some examples of "good" reasons for leaving former employers: desired a position which provided more opportunity for professional growth and continual self-development; company closed down operations; term position; seasonal employment; summer employment only; required more hours of work; required permanent part-time employment.

STEP 29: BUSINESS/CHARACTER REFERENCES

If you have excellent business or personal references, then by all means include them with your resume. Business references are names, titles, business addresses, and office telephone numbers of people who have employed you. Character references, on the other hand, are names, titles, business or home addresses, and office/home telephone numbers of people who have prominent positions or high profiles in your community (i.e., a doctor, lawyer, chartered accountant, person who owns their own business, school teacher, etc.). You might even consider asking your bank manager for a reference to indicate that your financial status is in good shape.

For an example of a good letter of reference, see Sample #15 in chapter 13. Perhaps one of your former employers would sign a letter like this one for you, if you asked him or her to.

If you can't secure any references at the moment, you could if necessary, say: "Available Upon Request."

STEP 30: ADDITIONAL REMARKS

At the end of your resume, you could stress how valuable a worker you are by including this final parting remark: "I am a results-oriented individual, and can work profitably, independently, or in cooperation with others. I work with enthusiasm and high energy on all assignments."

STEP 31: TITLE PAGE

If you have extensive business and\or professional experience, consider including a title page with your resume (see Sample #5). A title page can help give your resume a more corporate or professional look.

RESUME

Of

June Jobb
1011 Hunter Street
Albany, New York 12231
Home telephone: (518) 474-0000

WORKSHEET #1
RESUME WORKSHEET

RESUME WORKSHEET

1._____
     First name   Middle initial   Last name

2._____
     Apartment number   Street number   Street name

_____
     City   State/Province

_____
     zip or postal code

3. Home telephone: (area code)_____

Business telephone (area code)_____

Messages: (area code)_____

Fax: (area code)_____

4. PERSONAL INFORMATION

Birth date:_____(month/day/year)

Marital status: _____Dependents:_____

Height:_____Weight:_____

Health: excellent
     <u>Note</u>: I do not have a current or previous illness or disability that will affect my ability to perform the duties and responsibilities of this or any position.

Physical handicaps:none (If you have a physical handicap, leave this off your resume altogether.)

Citizenship:_____

Social Security/Insurance Number:_____

Driver's license number:_____

5. EDUCATIONAL BACKGROUND

_____, _____, _____, _____, _____
Degree   Name of college/university   City   State/Province   Year completed

Major:_____

Minor: _____

Diploma (Grade 12 academic/general): _____, _____,
     Name of school   City

_____, _____
   State/Province   Year completed

6. SPECIAL COURSES

_____, _____, _____, _____, _____
Name of course   Name of institution   City   State/Province   Year completed

Areas of concentration: (State in bullet form important aspects of the courses you studied)

- _____

- _____

- _____

- _____

7. WORKSHOPS AND SEMINARS

Name of workshop_____

Name of institution_____

_____
City   State/Province

Year taken_____

Lecturer: (only enter if individual is a prominent expert)_____

Duration:_____:

8. VOLUNTEER WORK

_____19 – ____ – 19 – ____   (month 19 – ____ month 19 – ___)

(Name of organization)_____

_____
(Street number and name),   (City, State/Province)

_____for this non-profit organization which_____
(Job or Position Title)   (define the role of this organization
                                                                           in the community).

9. SPECIAL LICENSES OR CERTIFICATES

_____   _____   _____ 19____
Name of certificate/license   Institution received from   (City, State/Province)   Date received

10. PROFESSIONAL AFFILIATIONS/SOCIETIES

_____   _____   _____ active member since 19___
Name of society   City   State/Province

11. UNION MEMBERSHIP

_____ member since 19 _____
Name of union

12. PATENTS/PUBLICATIONS

_____

13. SPECIAL SKILLS AND ABILITIES
- Possess strong interpersonal communication skills, and have a demonstrated interest in working harmoniously with others
- (See sample Resumes for other examples of what to say)

14. KNOWLEDGE OF LANGUAGES:

_____
(Name(s) of languages(s))

Reading ability:_____Writing ability:_____

Speaking ability:_____Comprehension ability:_____
                              (Enter as good, fair or excellent)

15. TRAVEL: Willing to comply with all travel requirements; own a car.

16. RELOCATE: Willing to relocate.

17. AVAILABILITY: Immediate *(or)* Minimum of two weeks' notice required.

18. PRESENT EMPLOYER: Present employer is prepared to discuss any questions regarding my work record at this time. (Please refer to the Business References provided at the end of this resume for the name, address, and business telephone of individual to contact).

(or)
PRESENT EMPLOYER: My present employer is currently unaware of my decision to seek other employment; however, he/she may be contacted to answer any questions about my work record, after first notifying myself of your intention to do so.

19. BONDABLE: I am bondable, and can pass a police security check.

20. SHIFTWORK: Willing to work shiftwork.

21. RESERVE DUTY: Willing to work on call twenty-four hours per day.
(or)
RESERVE DUTY: Willing to work on call in the absence of fellow employees or in the event of an emergency.

22. OVERTIME: Willing to work any amount of overtime.

23. SPECIAL TRAINING: Willing to undergo any amount of special training deemed necessary to more adequately meet the continuing demands of this position.

24. PROFESSIONAL INTERESTS:

_____

_____

25. HOBBIES AND INTERESTS:_____

_____

26. SALARY EXPECTED: Open — nature and challenge of position itself is of principal concern.
(or)
SALARY EXPECTED: Negotiable _____.

27. WORK EXPERIENCE

19____ – 19____: (Type of employment i.e., full-time, temporary, on-call, summer, etc.)

_____
(Name of Company)

_____
(Street number and name)

_____, _____
(City,   State/Province)

WORKSHEET #1 — Continued

_____

(Job Title Underlined)   (and definition of the company)

Reporting directly to the_____ principal duties involved the following:
                          (Supervisor's Title),

_____

_____

FIRST KEY RESPONSIBILITY: Responsible for_____
(Describe your specific contributions in this area using the sample resumes in the appendix for
assistance)

_____

_____

SECOND KEY RESPONSIBILITY: Responsible for _____
(Describe your specific contributions in this area using the sample resumes in the appendix for
assistance)

_____

THIRD KEY RESPONSIBILITY: Responsible for_____
(Describe your specific contributions in this area using the sample resumes in the appendix for
assistance)

_____

_____

Note: This position required an ability to work with confidence, accuracy, efficiency, and
understanding under all types of pressure situations; and throughout my employment, I consistently
scored high on all Performance Evaluations conducted by my employer.

28. REASON FOR LEAVING: Desire a position which provides more opportunities for professional
growth and continual self-development.

19___ – 19___: (Type of employment i.e., full-time, temporary, on-call, summer, etc.)

_____

(Name of Company)   (Street number and name) (City, State/Province)

_____

(Job Title Underlined)

Reporting directly to the_____ principal duties involved the following:
                          (Supervisor's Title),

_____

_____

FIRST KEY RESPONSIBILITY: Responsible for
(Describe your specific contributions in this area using the sample resumes in the appendix for
assistance)

_____

_____

SECOND KEY RESPONSIBILITY: Responsible for
(Describe your specific contributions in this area using the sample resumes in the appendix for
assistance)

_____

THIRD KEY RESPONSIBILITY: Responsible for
(Describe your specific contributions in this area using the sample resumes in the appendix for
assistance)

_____

_____

Note: This position required an ability to work with confidence, accuracy, efficiency, and
understanding under all types of pressure situations; and throughout my employment, I consistently
scored high on all Performance Evaluations conducted by my employer.

29. BUSINESS REFERENCE(S)

_____
(Name of Individual)   (Job Title)

_____
(Company employed by)

_____
(Street number and name)

_____
(City)   (State/Province)

_____
(Zip/Postal Code) — not important if a local address

Business telephone: (area code)_____-_____

CHARACTER REFERENCE(S)

_____
(Name of Individual)   (Job Title)

_____
(Company employed by)

_____
(Street number and name)

_____
(City)   (State/Province)

_____
(Zip/Postal Code) — not important if a local address

Home telephone: (area code)   _____-_____

Business telephone: (area code)_____-_____

30. ADDITIONAL REMARKS: I am a results-oriented individual and can work profitably, independently, or in cooperation with others; and I work with enthusiasm and high energy on all assignments.

_____

_____

_____

_____

_____

7

SPECIAL CASES

a. STUDENTS

Students or recent graduates face a catch-22 type of situation when they go job hunting. They want a job, but they are told the same discouraging story everywhere: "You don't have the necessary experience."

And, of course, the natural follow-up question is: "How are you supposed to get the necessary experience without first having a job?" It is a frustrating position to be in, but there is a way out.

If you do not have any substantial work experience, then what you must do is this: convince whoever has the hiring power in the organization you want to work for that —

(a) You have a clear understanding of what you are looking for in a job,

(b) You have a genuine interest in acquiring experience in all aspects of it.

Expressed another way: tell the employer your career objective.

Why do you want the job you are applying for? Is it desirable to you because you are out of work and anything that comes along in your direction must be applied for? Or do you have a very definite notion of what you want and for that reason alone you are going after it?

If it's the latter reason, you have a career objective. You know what the job you are after entails. You like those kinds of responsibilities and would appreciate being given an opportunity to do them. But the trick is to put your career objective into writing using terms of reference that the prospective employer can relate to.

For example, let's say you are a student who has graduated from grade 12 and wants to go into the air lines industry as a travel consultant. How would you break into this field? Well, for one thing, you would have to be able to identify the people in this field with hiring power (which is an impossible task in itself unless you know someone on the inside or have read chapter 10 in this book).

Secondly, you would have to have a convincing message to offer the person with hiring power about why you should be considered for a travel consultant position.

That convincing message is what the career objective is all about. Instead of saying to the prospective employer ill-considered things like: "I've always been interested in travel consultant work, ever since I was a little boy/girl," or "I think I'm interested in this field — my parents say I'd make a great travel consultant because of my natural ability to get along with people so well." Those are things that any of us could say with little or no thought. The person applying for travel consultant work would be much better off presenting the employer with a message like this one:

Career Objective: Desire a full-time travel consultant position which provides ample opportunities to learn and put into practice duties and responsibilities that are similar in nature to the following:

- Maintaining numerical, alphabetical and chronological files

- Preparing and mailing invoices to clients

- Interviewing customer complaints and ensuring prompt resolutions with the appropriate departments

- Interpreting policy and procedure issued from top management

- Interpreting tariff books and other technical publications

- Booking airfares

- Arranging itineraries

- Working out various types of fares to ensure the most economical route, as well as advising clients on a variety of levels (i.e., high or low seasons; midweek or excursion fares; high, moderate or affordable cruises; package tours, geography, climate, health requirements, visas, rental cars, hotels, theater tickets, etc.)

What does the above mentioned career objective say to the person with hiring power who ends up reading it? It says all of this:

(a) The job applicant (or person looking for work) has a complete understanding of the principal areas of responsibility that a travel consultant has.

(b) The applicant realizes that a travel consultant job is not all consultant work (i.e., some menial duties are also required, such as filing and mailing invoices).

(c) The applicant can distinguish the more demanding duties from the least demanding ones, as evident in the order in which the duties were listed.

(d) The applicant seems to be very interested in travel consultant work. (Who else would take the time to find out so much about this type of work except a person who is genuinely interested in it?)

(e) The applicant's stated ambitions are directly in line with the goal of our company (e.g., travel agency, airline company, etc.).

(f) The applicant has a definite notion of what he or she wants in a career.

You will set yourself apart from the rest of the job hunters by providing prospective employers with your career objective. How? You are not just handing in a resume of yourself (that contains little work experience to speak of) and aimlessly asking "What can you do for me, employer?" Instead, you are saying in clear speaking terms (terms that hit home with the employer's needs), "This is what I would like to have an opportunity to do for you."

How do you write a career objective? It's easy to do with the help of this book. Just read through the sample resumes. When you see a duty that looks like one you'd be expected to do (in your career choice), copy it down on a scrap of paper. Continue collecting these duties until a comprehensive list is put together. Then tailor it down to only significant responsibilities.

Once you know what you are going to use, enter it in type on a sheet by itself. The first duty you enter should be the least attractive one. And the last duty you enter should be the most attractive one (with all the ones in between becoming more and more attractive as one reads on). For instance, in the travel consultant career objective, the first duty mentioned is filing. That's the least attractive duty.

The most attractive one is "advising clients on a variety of levels" and that is entered last of all. In the middle is "interpreting policy and procedure" because it's more challenging than filing but at the same time less demanding than advising clients. You want to convey your willingness to learn. Do so by stressing the least appealing side of the job you want to secure.

Place your career objective between the title page of your resume and the resume itself.

b. THE MILITARY PERSON

If you have a lot of military experience to account for on your resume, before you begin writing consult your Unit Employment Record (U.E.R.).

Your U.E.R. contains most of the pertinent information you will need. For example, it will have courses taken, special qualifications, dates and locations of training programs and letters of commendation. However, it is not in a coherent form as is; because of this, you must put it in a readable form (i.e., your resume) for the prospective employer.

As you take what you need from your U.E.R., try to keep this one very important point at the center of all your thoughts: military words are like a foreign language to most people. So do your best to keep military terminology out of your resume. Admittedly, it is not all that easy to do. Especially when you consider that the military terms of reference you have been using for so long have become almost like a second language to you. But an over-dependence on military words when writing your resume will only confuse the civilian reading it.

Of course there will always be times when a military term needs to be used, such as when you are mentioning places you were stationed in. If you were stationed in St. Louis, Missouri, at the "United States Air Force Base," then what else can you say except that. Likewise, if you were aboard the "H.M.C.S. Provider" in Esquimalt, British Columbia, then that is what you need to say on your resume.

Another example of having to use military terminology could be your job classifications within the Armed Forces. If you were an operations officer, sergeant, leading seaman, able seaman, or ordinary seaman, then you would say that. There is no need to find a civilian equivalent here; no need to carry things to extremes. Just use a civilian term when you can.

Look at an example of over-using military terms and see what can be done to correct it.

How do you think a civilian employer would react to reading the following account of an operation officer's duties and responsibilities?

January 11, 1985 – present
H.M.C.S. Ojibawa
Halifax, Nova Scotia
Operations's Officer: Duties involve operating the SHIP in an ANTI-SUBMARINE ENVIRONMENT; training all SUBORDINATES within the OPERATIONS DEPARTMENT; coordinating the overall training requirements of the SHIP'S CREW; instructing JUNIOR OFFICERS in NAVIGATION and SHIP HANDLING; setting-up and implementing various MILITARY PROGRAMS concerned with the DEPLOYMENT OF SHIPS AT SEA; providing instructions to CREW members in MUNITIONS (i.e., ASROC MISSILES, GUIDANCE SYSTEMS, PROPULSION SYSTEMS and WARHEADS).

One way of getting around the problem of over-using military words is by realizing that it's the individual tasks you were responsible for that count to an employer, and not the environment in which it took place. For instance, the first duty in the above example stresses the environment (anti-submarine environment) rather than emphasizing the task of operating a ship itself. So does the second duty when it calls your attention to "within the operations department."

By continually stressing where the task was completed rather than just calling attention to the task itself you are putting yourself at a disadvantage in the job hunt. Why? Because a civilian employer who reads expressions like "deployment of ships at sea" is being reminded that you got your experiences through the military. Instead of giving complete attention to what your various skills and abilities are, and the relevancy these have to the position being offered, the employer is focusing more on "where" your skills and abilities were acquired than on "what" you have to offer. Leave out the military words and you will get a more objective analysis of your potential value as an employee.

A better way of describing the operations officer's duties would be like this:

January 11, 1985 – present
H.M.C.S. Ojibawa
Halifax, Nova Scotia
Operations Officer: Principal duties involve the following:
PROGRAM PLANNING: Responsible for setting up training programs for all personnel (i.e., formulating the description of proposed programs; delineating specific aims and objectives; determining the leadership requirements; forecasting costs and administrating program budgets; determining space, special equipment and facilities needed; formulating time schedules; establishing essential records and recording procedures; reviewing the results of programs in order to identify those areas where program aims and objectives have been successfully attained);
STAFF SUPERVISION: Responsible for interpreting top policy and procedure and ensuring staff compliance with directives; planning and scheduling of workloads; promoting a working environment that is conducive to greater learning and involvement; promoting a team approach to problem solving; promoting good housekeeping standards in order to ensure the occupational health and safety of all personnel; regularly acting in the absence of the Commanding Officer.

You can see that all military jargon (except the last duty mentioned) has now been carefully avoided. The last duty: "regularly acting in the absence of the Commanding Officer" can be left in because as mentioned before, there is no need to go to extremes.

To find the civilian phrases that best express your varied military background, simply read through all the sample resumes in this book. By doing so, you will find plenty of phrases that capture word-for-word exactly what you have done. In those instances where you can't find exactly the same task you did for the military, find one that closely approximates it and then modify it to suit your particular circumstances.

c. THE JOB HOPPER

If you have a scattered work record to account for on your resume, use a functional resume format to present it. A functional resume is exactly the same as a chronological resume except in one way. It covers up an inconsistent work record by holding back on the dates of employment.

For example, assume you had five years of experience as a mill mechanic. But also say that you didn't get these five years of mechanical experience all at one time. Instead, you spent a year at one company, two years at another, a year and one-half at another company and yet again a half a year at another company. Thus, over a five-year period you went through four jobs. Pretty scattered right? It would not look very impressive to an employer if you accounted for every one of them.

What you need to do in this type of situation is to gather all the jobs together and present them as one. For example:

Five years experience
Mill mechanic work
Atlanta, Georgia

Mill Mechanic: Duties and responsibilities involved the following: *(Enter your job description here)* _____

_____

_____

_____

When you put your work experience in a functional resume format, company names and addresses are left out, as well as various job titles. Everything is brought together into one neat package. Thus, you look less threatening to the prospective employer.

Whether or not you use a functional or chronological resume is up to you. Keep in mind that functional resumes still provide employers with a detailed analysis of your job experience in terms of what you actually did. They simply cover up the length of time you spent in each position.

d. THE VOLUNTEER: WORK EXPERIENCE THAT COUNTS

Did you ever stop to consider the advantages that come to you from doing volunteer work? There are many advantages, even though volunteer work is, by definition, something done for free. No money is exchanged for services rendered. However, whether or not you receive money for the work you do is irrelevant, as far as your job search campaign is concerned.

Work is work, and any knowledge and experience that you have earned along the way can be accounted for on your resume. So, with this in mind, let's have a look at some of the more important gains that come to you personally from doing volunteer work.

First of all, volunteer work gives you a golden opportunity to test out careers of interest to you. For instance, say that you are considering a career in social service work. But you are not sure about this kind of work. Well, one way of becoming more sure would be by doing volunteer work for an organization connected with social services. In volunteering your time to such an organization, you may discover certain realities about the nature of social service work that either confirm your desire to be

there or else force you into reconsidering your career plans.

Second, volunteer work could possibly pave the way for you to make the transition from non-paid work to paid work experience. For example, while doing volunteer work in any particular organization, you will have a chance to become acquainted with people with hiring power. If you impress these people with the quality and quantity of your work, you may eventually find yourself being invited to join their team on a full-time basis.

Third, volunteer work permits you either to acquire new work related strengths or brush-up on old ones. For example, anyone who is interested in acquiring basic training in secretarial work would be able to do so by volunteering their time in an office. Or if an individual already had skills in typing and filing, but felt a little rusty in these areas, then he or she could do volunteer work to improve speed and accuracy.

Fourth, if you are beginning to feel doubtful about your worth to employers, volunteer work could provide you with the boost in morale you may need to improve your self-esteem.

Fifth, maybe you are short of business and character references. If so, then volunteer work could help you establish the contacts you need with people who could vouch that you are highly motivated, clear in your intentions, and honest.

What kind of organizations are in need of volunteers? It is mainly non-profit organizations that use volunteers. Non-profit organizations are more apt to be understaffed than organizations that make profits. And because of this, they will in all likelihood extend a warm welcome to anyone who is willing to help out. Here are some examples of non-profit organizations that look for volunteers: fraternity clubs; lodges for the aged; community centers;

youth clubs; action leagues; research organizations; counselling societies; schools and colleges; activity centers; hospitals and mental health institutions; churches; fundraising groups; community television networks; correction centers; homemaker groups; museums; art galleries; theaters; etc.

Perhaps volunteer work already forms the bulk of your work record. If this is the case, here is a tip for you: enter your volunteer work on your resume as WORK EXPERIENCE and not as VOLUNTEER WORK EXPERIENCE. Why? Because there is no need to stress the fact that you were not paid for the work you did. All that the prospective employer needs to know is that you have the knowledge and experience necessary to adequately fill his or her job opening. Whether or not you were paid for your work is unimportant. If you volunteered your time to a non-profit organization, here is how you would set it up:

WORK EXPERIENCE
1990 – 1991: part-time work
Name of Organization
Street Address
City, State/Province
Job Title: (make up a job title if you were not given one)
Duties and responsibilities involved the following: ...

By presenting your volunteer work experience to an employer in this format, you will receive the kind of recognition that you deserve for the knowledge and experience you have acquired.

The best way of getting into volunteer work is by either directly approaching the non-profit organization that interests you most, or by making your intentions known at your local volunteer bureau. In either case, make sure you take along a copy of your resume. It will help the people you see in these organizations place you in the job that best meets your needs and their needs.

8

ADDING THE FINAL TOUCHES

As soon as you are sure about what information you intend to use on your resume, take some time to consider the following before preparing your master copy: the paper, the kind of type to use, computer typesetting, photocopying, the folder, and the envelope. All of these items can help create a favorable impression in the mind of the employer. Remember that the physical presentation of your resume is every bit as important as the actual message it contains.

a. THE PAPER

Paper comes in a wide assortment of sizes, shapes and colors. And the individual who is most aware of this fact is the employer. Every employer receives a variety of correspondence from not only job applicants but from business people, customers, etc., all the time. Therefore, they all have a very good idea about what good paper looks like.

The very best grade of paper for your resume is a brand called Classic Laid. Both the high cotton content and grainy texture of this paper combine to give the print on your resume an outstanding overall appearance. Most of your competitors in the job search will be using the regular 20 lb. stock of paper. You can buy Classic Laid paper in just about any stationery store or printing company (in boxes of 500 sheets or smaller quantities) and in all kinds of different colors.

The most attractive color (for resumes) is: Avon Brilliant White.

b. THE TYPEWRITER

After you have selected the grade of paper that pleases you most, the next step is to type your resume on it. Type your resume using one and one-half spaces between lines.

Keep in mind that there are only two kinds of typewriters on the market: good typewriters and very bad typewriters. The good ones are electric with carbon or film ribbons; the very bad ones are standard with ink ribbons.

The reason why standard typewriters are bad for typing your resume is because the letters from these machines get punched out on to the paper in different strengths. Occasionally a letter or two comes out on the paper strong and readable, but they will always be followed by letters that come out weak. You might even get smudged letters which, of course, will not make a very good impression.

The reason that electric typewriters with carbon or film ribbons are the ones you should be using for your resume is that all the typing comes out consistently crisp, clear and strong.

c. COMPUTER TYPESETTING

The very best way to have your resume typed is by using a computer with a laser printer, and anyone who has a business or professional background should strongly consider using this method. The computer, if it has a WordPerfect Program (or similar software package) allows you to:

(a) **bold**, or emphasize item headings on your resume in big, attractive letters,

(b) enter names of courses, workshops, etc. in *italics*,

(c) underline key ideas with <u>single</u> or <u>double</u> lines, and

(d) select the kind of type you like best. (See Resumes 4, 8, 18, and 23 for an example of a *sans serif* typeface, and Resumes 3, 19, and 37 for an example of a *serif* typeface.)

The Laser Printer ensures that the original copy of your resume is immaculate in its appearance. A resume typed in this way would strongly suggest to the employer that he or she is dealing with a person who has a very professional attitude towards their work.

To find someone who can type your resume on a computer using a laser printer, call up some companies in your area that sell computers. If they don't provide this kind of service to the public themselves, they may be able to recommend someone to you who can.

d. WHAT IF YOU CAN'T TYPE?

If you cannot type, find someone who can and pay for the service. The going rate varies and could be $10 or more per page, depending upon who you talk to. Why so high? Because typing a resume is more complicated and time-consuming than, say, typing an essay. There is a lot of work involved in knowing how to set it up properly.

In tracking down a typist (if you don't already know someone who can do it for you), check with the English Department of your local community college or university. Typists sometimes advertise their services in these places.

Another alternative is to get on the telephone to a local business firm and ask someone there if they could refer you to a good typist.

e. PHOTOCOPYING AND PRINTING

After typing your resume, find a good photocopier to do your duplicating. The best photocopy equipment is not found in your local post office or library but in a commercial firm. Even better than photocopying is quick printing, which is done on an offset press.

To find an offset press, look under "Printers" in the Yellow Pages of your telephone directory. Most printers have an offset press and also the Classic Laid paper to use for your resume.

Pull out the telephone numbers of several printers and call each one to find out the rates. You will be surprised how much their rates vary.

f. THE FOLDER

Hand your resume to an employer in a transparent report folder that is bound by a white plastic tension bar. These transparent plastic report folders (which are available in most stationery stores) are ideal for protecting your resume as well as contributing to the aesthetic quality of your overall presentation. If you check around, you will find that the prices for report folders vary, sometimes considerably, from store to store.

g. THE ENVELOPE

Buy a 9" x 12" white envelope to insert your resume in. There are two reasons for this —

(a) By using a 9" x 12" envelope you can put your resume into it without having to fold it into three parts, and

(b) White envelopes usually travel through the mail faster than brown ones.

9

COVERING LETTERS: WHAT ARE THEY AND WHO NEEDS THEM?

When you send your resume off to a particular organization that interests you, you should also send along a letter that explains (to the person receiving your resume) why you are contacting them. This letter is called a covering letter or letter of application.

If your resume is received by an employer unaccompanied by a covering letter, the employer has to ask, "Is this person applying for a particular job vacancy currently being advertised?" or "Is this person hoping I will keep this resume on file for future reference in case an opening does occur?" or "Is this person trying to call my attention to some special experience and ability that he or she would like to offer my organization?" In other words, the employer would appreciate knowing why you are writing before beginning to review your resume.

You can answer questions like the ones above in your covering letter. In one typewritten page, you say in the covering letter what position you are applying for (or would like to be considered for in the future) and why you feel you should be considered as a possibility for the job.

Keep in mind that in the covering letter you are only attempting to highlight the most important qualifications that you have for the job. All of the details (that persuade the employer of your true value) should be in the resume.

Sometimes you will read job advertisements in the newspaper that say "submit your application for employment in your own handwriting." By this the employer does not mean write your entire resume and covering letter in handwriting. The employer is simply saying to you that good handwriting is important for the job and because of this he or she would like to see a sample of yours. Employers also request handwritten applications for character analysis purposes. So fulfill this requirement by handwriting your covering letter.

If you are not specifically asked to "submit your application for employment in your own handwriting," then type both your covering letter and resume. Remember to put your hand signature on the covering letter at the bottom of the page just above where you type your name out in full.

Three different styles for writing your covering letter have been included in this book for your convenience. They are:

(a) block style, open punctuation,

(b) modified block style, open punctuation, and

(c) block style, alternate close punctuation.

There is no right style or wrong style or even one that is more popular than all the others. Just look them over and choose the one you like best.

Anyone who contacts a company through the mail rather than visiting it in person needs a covering letter. It is your formal introduction. If you intend to hand in your resume to the company in person (and know beforehand that you are having a personal interview with the prospective employer) then you could get by without one. In this type of situation you can clarify verbally what would otherwise be said in writing.

Sample #6 through #10 are examples of covering letters and should provide you with a reasonably good indication of what you should aim for in preparing your own letter. You will notice that some of these letters can be copied for your own use word-for-word. About the only things you will need to add are your name, the name of the newspaper you found the job opening in and the name of the person you are directing the letter to.

SAMPLE #6
MODIFIED BLOCK STYLE, OPEN PUNCTUATION

```
                              Gladys L. Powell
                              162 Washington Avenue
                              Albany, NY 12231

                              April 3, 1991

Department of Social Services
134 12th Avenue
Albany, NY 14331


To Whom It May Concern:

   I would appreciate your kindness in considering my application
for the position of Counselor as advertised in the NEW YORK POST,
April 2, 1991. I have enclosed a resume.

   You will notice that I have been successful in counseling spe-
cial needs children on problems pertaining to their home environ-
ment, social skills, and learning difficulties. I have also had
considerable experience in conducting psychological and educa-
tional evaluations.

   Should you wish to arrange a personal interview, I am willing
to come to your office at a time convenient to you.

   Thank you for your time, and I look forward with much pleasure
to hearing from you.



                              Sincerely yours,

                              Gladys L Powell

                              Gladys L. Powell
```

SAMPLE #7
BLOCK STYLE, ALTERNATE CLOSE PUNCTUATION

Lorraine C. Comeau,
1220 5th Avenue,
Gagnon, Quebec
G1R 4Y5
April 3, 1991

Employment Office, In-Flight Service,
Eagle Airway,
P.O. Box 345,
Gagnon, Quebec
G2R 2Y5

To Whom It May Concern:

I would appreciate your kindness in considering my application
for a Flight Attendant position with your airlines. A brief of my
background is enclosed.

You will notice that I have had considerable experience in working directly with the public as a waitress providing professional
service in first class restaurants situated in Gagnon.

As a waitress, I have been very successful in meeting deadlines
and handling pressure situations. I have also clearly demonstrated both to myself and to my employers that I have the
ability to work with confidence, accuracy efficiency, and understanding in all types of pressure situations.

Because of my considerable experience gained in service-oriented
businesses, and my language capabilities in both French and English, I believe that I could project an excellent company image
to your customers while most adequately fulfilling the demands of
a Flight Attendant position.

Your review of the enclosed details of my background will be
greatly appreciated. Should you wish to arrange a personal interview, I am willing to come to your office at a time convenient to
you.

Thank you for your valuable time, and I look forward to hearing
from you in the near future.

Very truly yours,

Lorraine C. Comeau

Lorraine C. Comeau

Encl: 1 Eagle Airway Application Form

SAMPLE #8
BLOCK STYLE, OPEN PUNCTUATION

```
                                    Catherine C. White
                                    546 Denver Street
                                    Madison, WI 51234
                                    April 30, 1991


Patricia Sherwood, President
Sherwood, Smith & Associates Ltd.
234 Ridge Street
Madison, WI 53707


Dear Ms. Sherwood:

Please consider my application for the position of Accountant as
advertised in the Madison Times, April 29, 1991. A brief resume
of my background is enclosed.

You will notice that I have been very successful in accounting,
and for this reason, I believe I could make an important contribu-
tion to your accounting firm.

Should you wish to arrange a personal interview, I would be happy
to meet with those concerned.

I look forward to your reply.


Respectfully yours,

Catherine C. White

Catherine C. White
```

Barbara L. Wamboldt
#103 - 5th Avenue
Toronto, Ontario
Z1P 0G0
May 21, 1991

Personnel Department
The Healall Hospital
24 Timesaround Avenue
Toronto, Ontario
Z1P 1Y0

To Whom It May Concern:

I am interested in acquiring a position as a Public Health Nurse
with your hospital. If such a position should become available in
the near future, I would appreciate your courtesy in considering
my application. My resume is enclosed.

You will notice upon reviewing my resume that I have been very
successful in this area, and for this reason, I believe that I
could most adequately fulfill the duties and responsibilities of
this kind of position.

Thank you for reviewing my enclosed resume. I would be happy to
meet with those concerned to discuss my application for employment.

Thank you for your valuable time.

Sincerely yours,

Barbara L. Wamboldt

Barbara L. Wamboldt

Encl. 2 letters of reference
       Transcript of university marks
       Assessment forms from Student Practicums

SAMPLE #10
COVERING LETTER IN RESPONSE TO AD

Lise A. Desrochers
123 Quadra Street
Tallahassee, FL 32301
July 21, 1991

Mr. Robert McEwen, Director of Teaching Personnel
Tallahassee School Board
P.O. Box 700
Tallahassee, FL 23301

Dear Mr. McEwen:

Please consider my application for the position of School Principal as advertised in the FLORIDA NEWSWEEK, July 19, 1991. My resume is enclosed.

You will notice that I have been successful in this area, and for
this reason, I believe that I could most adequately fulfill the
duties and responsibilities of this position.

Should you wish to arrange a personal interview, I would be happy
to meet with those concerned.

Thank you for your time, and I look forward to hearing from you
in the near future.

Yours truly,

Lise A. Desrochers

Lise A. Desrochers

10

GETTING A JOB INTERVIEW: UNCOVERING THE PERSON WITH HIRING POWER

a. DO YOUR OWN COMPANY RESEARCH

After your resume has been prepared, your next step involves learning how to use it to your best advantage. It's one thing to have purposeful communication about yourself, but it's quite another thing to know who should be reading it and how to get their attention.

Do you believe you can get good results by simply giving a copy of your resume to personnel officers at companies where you would like to work? How about responding to job advertisements in your local newspaper? Will that kind of strategy in itself eventually land you a good job? Would you give copies of your resume out to various employment agencies, and then sit back and wait for something good to happen? Or would you send your resume out to the top person in the organization you want to work for and have him or her assess your potential as an employee?

The last option would probably have the strongest appeal to you. When you have something worthwhile to offer an employer (i.e., a good work record and skills, abilities, knowledge and experience that you know the company can put to good use), why should you count on personnel officers, employment counselors, friends or business associates coming out in your most desperate moments to save you? All of these people may occasionally be useful contacts for you, but their help should be seen as a bonus and not as a principal source of assistance when looking for employment.

The most important individual who can help you in your search for employment is the employer in person. He or she is the one with the ultimate responsibility for hiring decisions made in the company. And this is the person you should be communicating with — whenever possible. "Yes," you say, "but just because I want to see the employer, it doesn't necessarily follow that the employer wants to see me."

True, but keep in mind that in making your availability for employment known to the employer, through your covering letter and resume, you are not imposing upon anyone. You are simply saying, "If you would like to see me I could meet with you at your convenience." If an employer does want to see you after reading your resume, it's entirely up to him or her.

The point being that the employer will decide if it's worth meeting you to discuss a job possibility, and not personnel officers, secretaries, or anyone else in the company.

But how do you get the key people in companies (especially the larger ones) to see your resume? Do you telephone the company you are interested in and ask whoever answers if you could have the President's or owner's name? No. The individual answering the telephone (who is probably the receptionist or another employee) would in all likelihood say, "May I ask who's calling please?" Then what will you do? Disclose your own identity and reason for calling so that the person talking to you can say things like: "We do all of our hiring through the personnel department," or "We are not looking for anyone now, but if you would like to come into the office you can fill out a standard application form," or some other equally discouraging remark.

There has to be a better way than this for identifying people with hiring power and for obtaining important insights on companies that interest you, and fortunately there is — but strangely enough, very few people know about it.

In the United States, you can find out who the key people are in companies by contacting the appropriate Bureau of Corporations (see section **b.**) located in the same state the prospective employer operates in.

In Canada, you can uncover who the key people are in any company, whether it's a proprietorship, partnership or limited company, by simply contacting the Registrar of Companies (see section **c.**) located in the same province the prospective employer operates in.

When you contact the appropriate bureau or registrar (either by telephone, in writing, or by fax) the representative will tell you who the key people are in any company that operates within that particular state or province. It's all that simple.

All you have to tell the bureau or registrar is the name of the company you are inquiring about. You don't even have to know the address of the company — just the name. The bureau or registrar will provide you with the names you are looking for — those with hiring power.

In the United States and Canada, both the Bureau of Corporations and the Registrar of Companies can not only tell you who the key people are, they will also tell you (depending on their particular state/provincial operating policies) other interesting things like —

(a) The home addresses of the employer and the chief people within the company (i.e., president, vice-president, board secretary and treasurer),

(b) What the business is (i.e., proprietorship, partnership, or limited company),

(c) The year in which the business was established as a proprietorship, partnership or limited company,

(d) The date of their last annual report (which tells you if the shareholders are being kept up-dated on company activities), and

(e) The most recent information they have on hand of that company's main activities (their reasons for being in existence as a company).

In other words, if you were living in Bangor, Maine, and were looking for employment as a photographer, this is what you would do:

(a) Prepare your resume according to the format given in this book.

(b) Turn to the Yellow Pages in the Bangor telephone directory and under the heading "Photographers," copy the names and addresses of several studios that interest you.

(c) Hop in your car or on a bus and go to all the studios to see the actual building (maybe enter it to get a sense of the overall atmosphere). Go back home with your general impressions.

(d) When you think you are sure about wanting to work for two or three of them, contact the bureau of corporation in Maine, by telephone, letter or fax. (See Sample #11.)

(e) Ask for the answers to the questions in Sample #12.

(f) Send your resume off to the employer's business address, using his or her correct title.

(g) Wait for a response (while you go through the same routine described above on other businesses that may be of interest to you).

In keeping with the same example, let's say that as a photographer you want to move from Bangor, Maine to Los Angeles, California (or any other city in the State of California). In this situation, all you would have to do is go to the public library in Bangor, Maine, haul out the Los Angeles telephone directory and look under the heading "Photographers" in the Yellow Pages. Copy down the names of studios that interest you and then contact the Bureau of Corporations in Sacramento, California for answers to your questions on these studios (see Sample #12.)

In Canada you would follow the same steps described above. Simply use the Yellow Pages of your telephone directory to find the names of the companies you would like to work for. Then, (see Sample #13) write or telephone the office of the Registrar of Companies located in the province the prospective employer operates in. Ask for the answers to those questions contained in Sample #14.

Thus you can see that regardless of where you live in the United States or Canada or where the companies are that you would like to work for, you can easily uncover the employer's name and valuable information about companies that interest you by contacting the appropriate state Bureau of Corporations or provincial Registrar of Companies. See sections **b.** and **c.** of this chapter for the address of the Bureau of Corporations or the Registrar of Companies in your state or province.

You may be billed for this service; however, it is a nominal charge. For example, in both Maine and New Brunswick the information is free. And in Toronto, Ontario, at the time of writing, the cost is $6 for each company you request information on.

Keep in mind that this exercise of contacting the Bureau of Corporations or Registrar of Companies is not just to find out the employer's name. It's also the most valuable means available to you for finding out important information about the company itself. For example, if you were asked at a job interview, "Do you know anything about our company?" how would you reply? If you had contacted the appropriate Bureau of Corporations or Registrar of Companies before going in for your interview, a question like this could be easily answered, and that would be very impressive for the employer to hear.

By the way, if the employer happens to ask you how you found out his or her name — and how you found out so many interesting facts about their operation — tell the truth. It's not top secret information. It's just that very few people (including employers themselves) realize that this sort of information is made public for the asking.

So don't just copy 25 names of companies at random from the Yellow Pages and then proceed to send your resume off to the key people.

Be careful about who you decide to contact. Only write to those employers who you believe could really benefit from your knowledge and experience.

SAMPLE #11
LETTER TO BUREAU OF CORPORATIONS

Lorraine C. Comeau
321 Kingsley Avenue
Bangor, ME 04222
January 12, 1992

Corporate Filing Division
Office of the Secretary of State
1230 J St.
Sacramento, CA 95814

To Whom It May Concern:

I would greatly appreciate your courtesy in helping me obtain answers to the enclosed questions regarding the following companies: Picture Perfect Studio, 123 Grafton Street, Sacramento, CA; Nu-Look Photography, #13 - 1700 Dundas Street, Sacramento, CA; Image Studio, 1111 Thurston Drive, Bakersfield, CA; Custom Photography, 1234 Mainshep Road, Alameda, CA; Perfect Color Photo Ltd., 65 McKowan Road, San Fernando, CA; Commercial Photographers, Clark Boulevard, Los Angeles, CA; and Team Photos Ltd., 799 Leading Road, Eureka, CA.

Please forward your fee for this service including any costs for photocopying pertinent memorandums and/or articles to the above address.

Thank you for your time and I look forward to hearing from you in the near future.

Yours truly,

Lorraine C. Comeau

Lorraine C. Comeau

Encl. List of questions

SAMPLE #12
QUESTIONS TO BUREAU OF CORPORATIONS (UNITED STATES)

I'd like to do a CORPORATE SEARCH on the following company(s)

Name of Company: _____

Address:_____

City/Province_____

1. Would you please provide me with the Charter Number in case I may need to refer to this file again?

_____

2. What is the most recent information you have on file about the purpose or main activities of this company (e.g., the nature of its services and/or products)?

_____

_____

3. Is this operation a limited company, financial institution, proprietorship, partnership, non-profit organization, or other?

_____

_____

4. Does this operation have branch offices, and if so, where are they located (e.g., city, street address, province)?

_____

_____

5. In what year did this operation become a limited company, financial institution, proprietorship, partnership, non-profit organization, or other?

_____

6. If this operation is a limited company, financial institution or non-profit organization would you please provide me with the most up-to-date information this file has on the names of those individuals who serve on the board of directors, their board titles, and their resident addresses?

(a)_____

_____

_____

(b) _____

_____

_____

(c)_____

_____

_____

7. If this operation is a proprietorship (or partnership), would you please tell me the name(s) of the owner(s) and their resident address(es)?

(a)_____

_____

(b)_____

_____

(c)_____

_____

8. Would you please provide me with the names, titles, and resident addresses of any officers in the company?

(a)_____

_____

(b)_____

_____

(c)_____

_____

9. What is the correct legal name of the company?

_____

10. Where is this company's records office located?

_____

11. Where is this company's registered office located?

_____

12. When did this company last file its annual report?

_____

13. Are there any encumbrances against this company?

_____

Thank you for your valuable time.

b. UNITED STATES: BUREAU OF CORPORATIONS

ALABAMA
Corporation Division
Office of Secretary of State
Room 524, State Office Bldg.
Montgomery, AL 36130
Telephone: (205) 242-5324

ALASKA
Corporation Section
Commerce & Economic
Development Dept.
P.O. Box D
Juneau, AK 99811
Telephone: (907) 465-2530

ARIZONA
Incorporating Division
Corporation Comm.
1200 W. Washington
Phoenix, AZ 85007
Telephone: (602) 542-3521

ARKANSAS
Secretary of State
Office of the Secretary of State
256 State Capitol Bldg.
Little Rock, AR 72201
Telephone: (501) 371-1010

CALIFORNIA
Corporate Filing Division
Office of the Secretary of State
1230 J St.
Sacramento, CA 95814
Telephone: (916) 324-1485

COLORADO
Division of Commercial Recordings
Department of State
1560 Broadway, Suite 200
Denver, CO 80203
Telephone: (303) 894-2251

CONNECTICUT
Corporations, UCC & Trademarks Div.
Office of Secretary of State
30 Trinity Street
Hartford, CT 06106
Telephone: (203) 566-2448

DELAWARE
Corporation Division
Department of State
Townsend Bldg.
Dover, DE 19901
Telephone: (302) 736-3073

FLORIDA
Corporate Records
Dept. of State
409 E. Gaines St.
Tallahassee, FL 32301
Telephone: (904) 487-6900

GEORGIA
Corporations Division
2 Martin Luther King, Jr. Dr., SE
Atlanta, GA 30334
Telephone: (404) 656-2806

HAWAII
Department of Commerce & Consumer
Affairs
1010 Richards Street
Honolulu, HI 96813
Telephone: (808) 548-7505

IDAHO
Secretary of State
Statehouse
Boise, ID 83720
Telephone: (208) 334-2300

ILLINOIS
Office of Secretary of State
328 Centennial Bldg.
Springfield, IL 62756
Telephone: (217) 782-6961

INDIANA
Corporation Section
Office of Secretary of State
155 State House
Indianapolis, IN 46204
Telephone: (317) 232-6587

IOWA
Office of Secretary of State
2nd Floor, Hoover Bldg.
Des Moines, IA 50319
Telephone: (515) 281-5204

KANSAS
Secretary of State
2nd Floor, State House
Topeka, KS 66612
Telephone: (913) 296-2236

KENTUCKY
Secretary of State
State Capitol Bldg.
Frankfort, KY 40601
Telephone: (502) 564-3490

LOUISIANA
Secretary of State
Department of State
P.O. Box 94125
Baton Rouge, LA 70804-9125
Telephone: (504) 925-4704

MAINE
Bureau of Corporations
State House Station #101
Augusta, ME 04333
Telephone: (207) 289-3501

MARYLAND
Department of Assessments & Taxation
301 W. Preston Street, Rm. 806
Baltimore, MD 21201
Telephone: (301) 225-1184

MASSACHUSETTS
Secretary of the Commonwealth
State House, Rm. 337
Boston, MA 02133
Telephone: (617) 727-2800

MICHIGAN
Corporations & Securities Bureau
Department of Commerce
P.O. Box 30222
Lansing, MI 48909
Telephone: (517) 334-6212

MINNESOTA
Corporations Division
Office of Secretary of State
180 State Office Bldg.
St. Paul, MN 55155
Telephone: (612) 296-2803

MISSISSIPPI
Corporations Division
Office of Secretary of State
401 Mississippi Street
Jackson, MS 39201
Telephone: (601) 359-1350

MISSOURI
Office of Secretary of State
Truman Bldg.
P.O. Box 778
Jefferson City, MO 65102
Telephone: (314) 751-4194

MONTANA
Corporations Bureau
Office of Secretary of State
State Capitol
Helena, MT 59620
Telephone: (406) 444-3665

NEBRASKA
Secretary of State
Rm. 2300, State Capitol
P.O. Box 94608
Lincoln, NE 68509-4608
Telephone: (402) 471-2554

NEVADA
Secretary of State
Capitol Complex
Carson City, NV 89710
Telephone: (702) 885-5203

NEW HAMPSHIRE
Secretary of State
204 State House
Concord, NH 03301
Telephone: (603) 271-3242

NEW JERSEY
Division of Commercial Recordings
Department of State
820 Bear Tavern Rd., CN 308
Trenton, NJ 08625
Telephone: (609) 530-6412

NEW MEXICO
Corporations Department
Corporations Comm.
P.O. Drawer 1269
Santa Fe, NM 87504-1269
Telephone: (505) 827-4508

NEW YORK
Secretary of State
Department of State
162 Washington Avenue
Albany, NY 12231
Telephone: (518) 474-4750

NORTH CAROLINA
Corporations Attorney
Corporations Div.
Office of Secretary of State
300 N. Salisbury Street
Raleigh, NC 2703-5909
Telephone: (919) 733-4201

NORTH DAKOTA
Corporation Division
Office of Secretary of State
1st Fl., State Capitol
600 E. Blvd.
Bismarck, ND 58505
Telephone: (701) 224-3669

OHIO
Office of the Secretary of State
30 E. Broad St. 14th Fl.
Columbus, OH 43266-0418
Telephone: (614) 466-3084

OKLAHOMA
Secretary of State
101 State Capitol
Oklahoma City, OK 73105
Telephone: (405) 521-3911

OREGON
Corporation Div.
Secretary of State
158 12th St. NE
Salem, OR 97310
Telephone: (503) 378-4383

PENNSYLVANIA
Corporation Bureau
Department of State
308 N. Off. Bldg.
Harrisburg, PA 17120
Telephone: (717) 787-1379

RHODE ISLAND
Corporation Div.
Office of Secretary of State
Smith Street
Providence, RI 02903
Telephone: (401) 277-3040

SOUTH CAROLINA
Secretary of State
P.O. Box 11350
Wade Hampton Bldg.
Columbia, SC 29211
Telephone: (803) 734-2155

SOUTH DAKOTA
Secretary of State
Capitol Bldg., 2nd Fl.
Pierre, SD 57501
Telephone: (605) 773-3537

TENNESSEE
Div. of Corporations
Office of Secretary of State
5th Fl., James K. Polk Bldg.
Nashville, TN 37219
Telephone: (615) 741-2286

TEXAS
Corporate Div.
Office of Secretary of State
Box 13697, Capitol Station
Austin, TX 78711
Telephone: (512) 463-5586

UTAH
Division of Corporations
Dept. of Business Regulation
160 E. 300 S.
Salt Lake City, UT 84111
Telephone: (801) 530-6027

VERMONT
Corporations Div.
Office of Secretary of State
26 Terrace St.
Montpelier VT 05602
Telephone: (802) 828-2386

VIRGINIA
State Corporation Comm.
1220 Bank St., 13th Fl.
Richmond, VA 23219
Telephone: (804) 786-3603

WASHINGTON
Corporate Div.
Office of Secretary of State
505 E. Union
M/S: PM-21
Olympia, WA 98504
Telephone: (206) 753-7120

WEST VIRGINIA
Secretary of State
State Capitol
Charleston, WV 25305
Telephone: (304) 345-4000

WISCONSIN
Corporations Div.
Office of Secretary of State
P.O. Box 7846
Madison, WI 53707
Telephone: (608) 266-3590

WYOMING
Corporations Div.
Office of Secretary of State
State Capitol
Cheyenne, WY 82002
Telephone: (307) 777-7311

DISTRICT OF COLUMBIA
Corporations Div.
Department of Consumer &
Regulatory Affairs
614 H St., NW, Rm. 407
Washington, DC 20001
Telephone: (202) 727-7278

GUAM
Department of Revenue & Taxation
855 W. Marine Drive
Agana, GU 96910
Telephone: (671) 477-5143

NORTHERN MARIANA ISLANDS
Registrar of Corporations
Off. of Attorney General
Saipan, MP 96950
Telephone: (670) 322-4311

PUERTO RICO
Secretary of State
Department of State
Box 3271
San Juan, PR 00904
Telephone: (809) 722-2121

U.S. VIRGIN ISLANDS
Office of Lt. Governor
18 Kongens Gade
St. Thomas, VI 00802
Telephone: (809) 774-2991

c. CANADA: REGISTRAR OF COMPANIES

FEDERAL

Corporations
Department of Consumer and Corporate
Affairs
4th Floor, Phase II
Ottawa-Hull, ON
K1A 0C9
Telephone: (819) 997-1058
Telephone: (819) 997-1142

BRITISH COLUMBIA
Ministry of Corporate Affairs
Companies Office
940 Blanshard Street
Victoria, BC
V8W 3E6
Telephone: (604) 387-5101

ALBERTA
Department of Consumer & Corporate
Affairs
Registrar of Corporations
10365-97 Street
8th Floor
Edmonton, AB
T5J 3W7
Telephone: (403) 427-2311

SASKATCHEWAN
Consumer & Commercial Affairs
Corporations Branch
1871 Smith Street
2nd Floor
Regina, SK
S4P 3V7
Telephone: (306) 787-2962
Telephone: (306) 787-9050

MANITOBA
Corporations & Business Names Branch
10th Floor,
504 Broadway Avenue
Winnipeg, MB
R3C 3L6
Telephone: (204) 945-5999

NEWFOUNDLAND
Registrar of Deeds, Companies &
Securities
Confederation Building, East Block
P.O. Box 4750
St. John's, NF
A1C 5T7
Telephone: (709) 576-3301
Telephone: (709) 576-3302

NORTHWEST TERRITORIES
Registrar of Legal Registries
Department of Justice
Government of the N.W.T.
P.O. Box 1320
Yellowknife, NT
X1A 2L9
Telephone: (403) 920-8985

ONTARIO
Ministry of Consumer and
Commercial Relations
393 University Avenue
2nd Floor
Toronto, ON
M7A 2H6
Telephone: (416) 596-3725
Telephone: (416) 596-3757

QUEBEC
Bureau de L'Inspecteur General des
Institution Financieres
800 Place d'Youville
Quebec, PQ
G1R 4Y5
Telephone: (418) 643-5253

NEW BRUNSWICK
Corporate and Trust Affairs
Department of Justice
P.O. Box 6000
670 King Street
Room 475
Fredericton, NB
Telephone: (506) 453-2703

NOVA SCOTIA
Registrar of Joint Stock Companies
1660 Holles Street
Main Floor
Halifax, NS
B3J 2Y4
Telephone: (902) 424-7770

PRINCE EDWARD ISLAND
Director of Corporations
Corporations Division
Department of Justice
Shaw Building
73 Rochford Street
P.O. Box 2000
Charlottetown, PE
C1A 7N8
Telephone: (902) 368-4550

YUKON
Administrator of Corporate Affairs
Department of Consumer & Corporate
Affairs
P.O. Box 2703
Whitehorse, YT
Y1A 2C6
Telephone: (403) 667-5225

SAMPLE #13
LETTER TO COMPANY REGISTRAR (CANADA)

Laura T. Ladd
1234 5th Street
Toronto, Ontario
M7B 2H6

Ministry of Consumer and Commercial Relations
393 University Avenue
2nd Floor
Toronto, Ontario
M7A 2H6

To Whom It May Concern:

I would greatly appreciate your courtesy in helping me obtain answers to the enclosed questions regarding the following companies: Portrait Studio, 123 Grafton Street, Toronto, Ontario; Sharp Photography, #13 - 1700 Dundas Street, East Mississauga, Ontario; Harrington's Photography, 1111 Thurston Drive, Ottawa, Ontario; Brandon's Photography, 1234 Mainshep Road, Weston, Ontario; Snapshot Studio, 65 McKowan Road, Scarborough, Ontario; Gloss Photographers, Clark Boulevard, Brampton, Ontario; and Perfect Print Photos Ltd., 799 Leading Road, Rexdale, Ontario.

Please forward your fee for this service including any costs for photocopying pertinent memorandums and/or articles to the above address.

Thank you for your time and I look forward to hearing from you in the near future.

Yours truly,

Laura T. Ladd

Laura T. Ladd

Encl. List of questions

SAMPLE #14
QUESTIONS TO COMPANY REGISTRAR (CANADA)

I'd like to do a FILE SEARCH on the following company(s)

Name of Company:_____

Address:_____

City/Province_____

1. Would you please provide me with the registration number (or incorporation number) in case I may need to refer to this file again?

\# _____

2. What is the most recent information you have on file about the main activities of this company (e.g., the nature of its services and/or products)?

_____

_____

3. Is this operation a proprietorship, partnership, limited company, non-profit organization or other?

_____

_____

4. Does this operation have branch offices, and if so, where are they located (e.g., city, street address, province)?

_____

_____

5. In what year did this operation become a proprietorship, partnership, limited company, non-profit organization, or other?

_____

_____

6. If this operation is a proprietorship (or partnership), would you please tell me the name(s) of the owner(s) and their resident address(es)?

_____

_____

_____

_____

7. If this operation is a limited company or non-profit organization would you please provide me with the most up-to-date information this file has on the names of those individuals who serve on the board of directors, their board titles, and their resident addresses?

(a)_____

_____

_____

(b)_____

_____

(c)_____

_____

8. Would you please provide me with the names, titles, and resident addresses of any officers in the company?

(a)_____

_____

(b)_____

_____

(c)_____

_____

9. What is the correct legal name of the company?_____

10. Where is this company's records office located? _____

_____

11. Where is this company's registered office located?_____

_____

_____

12. When did this company last file its annual report?_____

13. Are there any encumbrances against this company?_____

_____

_____

Thank you for your valuable time.

11

EMPLOYER VS. EMPLOYEE: FEAR IS THE COMMON DENOMINATOR

Both you and the prospective employer have lots to worry about when you are sitting in the same room with each other face to face during the job interview process.

You are worried (sometimes to the point of actual sickness) about what the employer is going to ask you during this meeting. The employer is worried about the possibility of having to experience a loss of valuable time, money, and mental energy if the wrong person is selected for the job opening.

Let's briefly examine the reasons behind both your fear, and the employer's fear of the job interview.

Before the employer calls anyone in for a job interview, there is a lot of initial preparation to go through. First of all, a job description must be prepared. That is to say, the employer must briefly outline what the duties and responsibilities are of the position that has become available in the company. The responsibilities must not look too challenging for fear of scaring off good candidates; at the same time, the duties must not look too easy since this would only encourage too many people without the necessary qualifications to apply.

After the employer is completely satisfied with the description of the available position, the next step is to test it. This is done by putting the job description in a newspaper. The kind of newspaper used (i.e., local, national, trade magazine, etc.) to advertise in will depend mainly upon the kind of readership the employer hopes to attract and the nature of the job itself. In any case, purchasing advertising space is expensive business. And it gets progressively more expensive as you go from local to national newspapers.

Then the employer is faced with the myriad of resumes that come flowing in as a result of the ad. There are long ones, short ones; neat ones, messy ones; ones that can be understood, ones that can't be understood; ones that have the qualifications; ones that don't have the qualifications; resumes that contain only job related information, resumes that contain no job related information; and so on.

Perhaps out of the flood of resumes the employer receives none of the candidates (wishful thinkers) have the necessary qualifications. This means the employer is at fault. The job description must have appeared too easy. So, back to the drawing board to write another description and then back to the newspaper to test it again. More money and time down the tubes.

On the other hand, maybe the employer's job description looks too challenging to the would-be employee and only a handful respond. So once again it's back to creating another job description because the employer knows more people should have answered the advertisement.

The employer who does get a good collection of candidates from the newspaper advertisement of the job must then make up a shortlist of applicants to interview and invite them in for an interview. This is another time-consuming activity since people are not always at home when you phone them.

Then, of course, there is the job interview itself. In order for it to be a success (i.e., a productive exchange of information), the employer must know in advance what questions to ask applicants. These are questions that probe more deeply into the candidate's background and bring out enlightening material that is not evident on the resume.

When at last the interviews with all those who made the shortlist are over, the employer must take the necessary time away from the company's problems to compare and contrast all the candidates with each other. This is another time-consuming and anxiety ridden task.

Upon finally deciding who to hire, the employer faces the time and expense of orienting the new employee to the business. This means giving the new recruit adequate time to become acquainted with the work environment and other staff members; time to explain company policy on such matters as codes of professional conduct and dress, dimensions of the job, specific accountabilities, benefit plans, sick leave and leave of absence, lateness, safety, etc. There may even be a formal training period that the new employee must undergo to better handle the new position. In any case, until the new recruit is capable of performing the job responsibilities at the expected level, the employer is up against an overall loss of productivity.

If the new employee cannot adequately handle the duties and responsibilities after a sufficient amount of time has been granted, he or she must be let go. This creates a very unpleasant situation for both the employer and the one who is getting fired. But it is more than just unpleasant for the employer; the employer must once again go through all the steps mentioned above, this time hoping to make the correct decision on who to hire.

So you can see that employers have plenty of reasons to fear job interviews. A lot of time, mental energy and money can be lost if he or she selects the wrong job applicant for the position.

You have plenty of justifiable reasons to fear job interviews too. But your fears come primarily from not knowing what kind of questions to expect during those 30 or so minutes and not knowing whether one person will be interviewing you or several people.

Although you can never know for sure how many people will be interviewing you, you can know in advance what kinds of questions to expect. And that's the reason for the next chapter.

12

INTERVIEW QUESTIONS: HOW TO PLAY THE ARTFUL DODGER

This chapter contains a list of questions that are most commonly asked of job applicants by employers, as well as the reasons why such questions are asked. Study them and then write down your best answer to each one. In this way you can substantially reduce the fears you might otherwise experience during the job interview.

Roughly speaking, there are three main areas of concern on the mind of every job interviewer about the applicant. They are:

(a) Will the candidate remain with our company for a reasonable length of time?

(b) Will the candidate work compatibly with our other staff members?

(c) Will the candidate make a strong contribution to our company's goals?

Or, in other words, is the job applicant a loyal, congenial, and hard working person?

To find out the answer to whether or not you are a loyal, congenial and hard working person, the employer will put you through a series of questions during the job interview.

For 45 minutes or more (depending on the position you are applying for), you will be asked questions that are designed to uncover things such as how motivated you are; how much potential you have for the job; how suitable your career choice is; how emotionally stable you are, etc.

In giving your answers to the employer, you should make a special effort not to repeat your resume statements. Your resume has already served its purpose and now you must introduce fresh information on your background into the discussion.

It is vitally important that you make the job interview as productive an exchange of information as you can. One of the main reasons why job applicants fail to convince employers of their true employable value is because they give only "yes" and "no" answers to the interview questions. The prospective employer needs facts to base the final decision on; and these facts have to come directly from you.

Remember that by the time you have been called in for a job interview, you are far ahead of nearly all the other applicants. Sure, there are a few people that the employer also intends to interview — people who have backgrounds that look as good as yours on paper.

But as far as the employer knows you would all make excellent employees. The employer is having problems at this stage trying to decide who to hire. And this is the reason why you are being called in for a job interview — to help break the deadlock.

Go into the job interview with the intention of breaking the deadlock in your favor. How? By studying the following questions carefully and then writing down your best answers to each one.

These questions or variations of them are very popular among job interviewers. If you are prepared with answers on all of them, there shouldn't be any problems for you during the job interview.

1. What are you looking for from this job?

The employer is looking for evidence of how motivated you are. For example, how great is your desire for responsibility and a sense of personal accomplishment?

2. What are your reasons for choosing this particular field of employment?

The employer hopes to discover how appropriate or inappropriate your career decision is. This is not an important question if you have been employed in a particular occupation for many years.

3. What personal qualities do you feel you have that make you suitable for this line of work?

The employer is trying to peg down some of your basic personality traits. It's a difficult question to answer. You may feel that being tough with people is what makes you great for the job, but the employer may see diplomacy as a more important human quality.

4. What do you think your strongest points are for this job?

This is a common question at job interviews. The employer hopes to see whether or not you are a braggart, and also, how quick you are on your feet. It's a tricky question to answer when you are not prepared for it. Be modest in your reply.

5. What would you say your weakest points are for this job?

(Usually question 4. is eventually followed by this one.) Answer it by saying something that sounds self-critical but nothing to get excited about. For example: "I like my work so much it slightly annoys my friends to hear me talk about it. But they are learning to accept this side of me."

6. Why did you choose our particular organization to work in?

This kind of question begs you to say something about the organization itself. You know how to research a company from reading chapter 10. So tell the employer what you know about the company's products/services, while at the same time providing your reason for desiring to work there.

7. What did you like least/most about former employers?

The employer wants an indication of how you judge others, i.e., fairly or in a derogatory manner. It is best not to say anything critical about a former employer.

8. What reasons could you offer to explain how someone might fail/succeed in carrying out the responsibilities of this job?

Your answer reveals the adequacy of your past work experience for the present job. If you are good at a particular job, then you should know what would constitute success or failure in executing the duties and responsibilities.

9. In terms of your career, where do you hope to be five years from now?

Your answer may reveal that you want to stay with the company for a long time upon being hired and that you are looking forward to being promoted within the company ranks someday.

10. If you could have had any job in your life, what would you have picked?

See question 2. Again, the employer is trying to discover how appropriate or inappropriate your career decision is.

11. Do you have any personal obligations that may limit your ability to perform the duties and responsibilities of this job?

The employer is trying to find out if your spouse, children, personal debts, etc. may have a negative influence on your job. Thus, an answer that implies you are happily married and in good financial standing should alleviate these concerns.

12. Do you have any physical or health problems that may affect your ability to do this job?

The employer wants to be assured that you haven't had any illnesses or accidents that were serious and that your personal physician would approve of you having this job.

13. What was the most complex on-the-job challenge that you have had to wrestle with?

The employer is looking for what you can say about your self-reliance in making decisions and resourcefulness in new and trying situations.

14. How would you deal with someone who has different ideas about the way things should be done?

The employer is interested in knowing whether or not you have the capacity to handle criticism from fellow workers and supervisors, as well as how you would express your own opinions, i.e., aggressively, passively, or moderately.

15. Do you mind working alongside of people who are not of the same ethnic or socio-economic background as yourself?

The employer wants to get some indication from you that you are capable of working in an objective manner, free from personal prejudice.

16. How would you handle a complaining customer?

The employer hopes to be able to assess how thorough a thinker you are by your response.

17. How do you think an employer should go about getting cooperation from all staff members?

The employer wants to see how you would give and take orders; how you would use or abuse delegated power; and whether or not you could promote high performance standards. Thus your answer should assure the employer that you can promote a team approach in the implementation and management of the company's goals, objectives and processes.

18. Tell me about yourself?

Tell the employer about a few things you have done in the past that indicate that your attitude, character, integrity, general upbringing, leadership abilities, personality, etc. suit you for the job.

19. Do you have any questions?

Play the role of the artful dodger right to the end of the job interview. Ask only questions that will show your concern for the employer's needs. For ideas on what you can ask, read through the questions that you will see in chapter 14.

One thing you may have noticed about all the above questions is this: they are all job related. That is to say, all the above questions try to reveal how adequate (or inadequate) the job applicant's knowledge and experience is for the position he or she is applying for.

Besides the above questions, there are many non-job related questions that can be asked of you as well. Some of the non-job related questions can be obnoxious and even a violation of your civil or human rights. A cross-section of these non-job related questions is listed below. Maybe you would rather avoid working for a company that would probe into such personal areas.

Whatever your position may be, there is no harm in acquainting yourself with these possibilities. So here are a few of them:

1. Have you ever received any speeding tickets in the last 12 months?

2. How do you spend your Sundays?

3. Do you provide entertainment in your home very often?

4. Do you have a girlfriend/boyfriend?

5. Do you have any personal debts?

6. Do you have any mental, emotional, or physical disabilities?

7. Do you attend church regularly? If so, which one?

8. Name a political or religious leader you admire?

9. Do you belong to any religious or political clubs or organizations?

10. Are there any religious holidays you observe?

11. What kind of books do you enjoy reading?

12. Do you drink?

13. Which one of your parents had the most profound influence on your overall development?

14. What was your home life like?

15. What is your marital status?

16. Were you ever divorced?

17. Do you have any savings?

18. Have you ever had your wages garnisheed?

19. Have you ever applied for credit and been refused?

20. What is your mother's and father's educational background and occupation?

21. Where do your ancestors come from?

22. Would you show us your birth certificate before we decide to hire you?

23. Have you ever had a criminal record for which a pardon has been granted?

24. Were you ever arrested?

25. Do you live in an apartment or own your own home?

26. How old are you?

27. Are you married?

28. Are you pregnant?

29. Are you planning to have any children?

30. Do you have any dependents?

31. Why did you leave school?

32. How did you support yourself while going to school?

13

DECISION TIME: HOW THE EMPLOYER FIGURES YOU OUT AFTER THE INTERVIEW

After the job interview is over, the employer will go through a series of objective and subjective evaluations before finally deciding who he or she is going to hire.

The subjective side of the evaluation will be more like guessing your probabilities of success on the job than applying any kind of logical principles. The employer will consider your personality, your intelligence (as revealed in your interview statements) and your manner of expression. He or she will play the role of the amateur psychiatrist in assessing your character, and sooner or later some innate feeling will temporarily take charge and say: hire the one whose personal conduct and outward appearances seemed most suitable for the job.

But experience has taught the most circumspect employer that appearances are often deceiving. Some people are very good actors; and those who just seem to be good prospects as employees are usually the ones who do not work out.

So here the objective side of the employer's reasoning steps into the action. It points out to the employer the dangers of reading too much between the lines. The objective side of the employer's evaluation focuses on things that can be measured: the consistency of your past work record; the extent of your educational background and technical knowledge bearing on the job; your income levels in past jobs; the number and kind of special awards you may have received in recognition of your past performance, etc.

Both the objective and subjective sides of the employer's evaluation of you will be competing for control. Either side could win. All you can do as a job applicant is become aware of what an employer is looking for in prospective employees and do your best to deliver it.

Therefore, review the following questions. They should give you a reasonably good idea of the kind of questions employers are apt to ask themselves before deciding who to hire.

1. Are the candidate's reasons for leaving former employers reasonable?

2. Are there any unexplained gaps in the candidate's work record?

3. Has the candidate gone through too many jobs in too short a time period?

4. Does the candidate have any health complications which may hinder his or her ability to perform on the job?

5. Is the candidate's previous income level in line with our wage offering?

6. Are most of the candidate's claims on his or her resume verifiable against outside sources?

7. Does the candidate have good business and personal references and are they legitimate? (Sample #15 on page 74 is an example of a letter of reference for an outstanding employee.)

8. How does the candidate's last employer rate him or her as a worker?

9. Does the candidate's resume show that he or she has the necessary experience (and related experience, e.g., volunteer work) for the job?

10. Are the candidate's grammar and vocabulary adequate for the job?

11. Were there any contradictions in the applicant's statements during the job interview?

12. Will the candidate work overtime when necessary?

13. Are the candidate's personal objectives as stated on the resume (or covering letter) and revealed during the job interview, compatible with our company's goals?

14. Does the applicant agree to accept a position within the company at another location?

15. Will the candidate participate in further on-the-job training, if necessary?

16. Does the candidate have a working knowledge of the jargon used by the company employees?

17. Does the candidate seem to have the emotional stability necessary for coping with unusual pressures on the job?

18. How does the candidate rank against those currently employed within the company doing the same work?

19. Does the candidate's contribution to past employers indicate anything significant about his or her probable future contribution to our company?

20. Will the candidate's need for occupational growth and personal self-development be met by this job?

21. Does the candidate dress neatly and take pride in his/her personal appearance and grooming?

22. Does the candidate seem capable of working well independently?

23. Did the candidate seem thoughtful and alert during the job interview?

24. Is the candidate's ability to articulate his or her ideas impressive?

25. Does the candidate's confidence, poise and maturity suit him or her for the job?

26. Does the candidate's overall manner suggest he or she may not work well with others?

27. Does the candidate seem amicable?

28. Does the candidate seem mature and honest?

29. Does the candidate seem highly motivated and enthusiastic?

30. Does the candidate seem to be going to "any port in the storm" or is he or she genuinely interested in this job?

31. Does the candidate seem to have the potential to be promoted when necessary?

32. Will the candidate be a thorough and accurate worker?

Ulysses Travel Agency
1133 St. George Boulevard
Edmonton, Alberta
Telephone: (403) 427-0000
Fax: (403) 427-1111

To Whom It May Concern:

This is to certify that Yolande M. Tour has been employed as a Travel Consultant with our company from June 23, 1983 – January 1991.

This position calls for a great deal of initiative, and we always found Ms. Tour to be highly courteous in the manner in which she dealt with our clients and most efficient in carrying out the various duties and responsibilities assigned to her. She also proved herself to be very successful in meeting deadlines and handling pressure situations.

I am sure that anyone requiring Ms. Tour's services will find her most willing to devote herself to the best interest of her employer, and for this reason, I do not hesitate in recommending her to your attentive consideration as she has been a great asset to our agency.

We wish her well in the pursuit of her career goals, and hope that she will feel free in quoting our company as a reference when furthering her career.

Yours truly,

John Foreman

John Foreman, President

14

JOB ANALYSIS:
HOW DO YOU KNOW YOU WANT THIS JOB ANYWAY?

Just as the prospective employer is evaluating you after the job interview, you should be appraising the employer and the job offering.

How do you feel about this person who will be paying you your salary? Does the overall environment of the firm you will be spending eight hours or more per day in seem warm and friendly or cold and unpleasant? In other words, how do you know you even want this job you are applying for?

Unfortunately, many people discover the true nature of the job they have accepted well after they have been hired. And if the realities of their job are not quite what they expected, the problems begin: ulcers, high blood pressure, anxiety attacks and heart attacks as well as other bodily and mental symptoms arising from an inability to adjust to the stresses and strains of the work environment.

Of course, if things were really bad, you could always quit. But do you really want to put yourself through all that time and trouble of having to find work again, and so soon?

Before jumping into your next job, ask yourself a few questions about it.

"What is there to ask?" you say. The job is there waiting for you; if you do not take it someone else will. The salary looks good; the job responsibilities appear challenging. There is even an attractive health care plan and room for advancement within the company ranks. "What more," you ask, "could a person want?"

Have a look. Below are the questions you need to ask yourself before accepting a job offer.

1. Will your personal needs be met by this job?

While employed within a particular business maybe you may need: long-range financial security; modern equipment to work on; opportunities for advancement within the company ranks; contact with other people; competition with fellow workers; a sense of personal achievement; a pleasant physical environment; or perhaps the freedom to work independently. Whatever you define as your needs you must critically question yourself as to whether or not this job can fulfill them.

2. Is the prospective employer's business well established or has it just recently been formed?

The Bureau of Corporations or Registrar of Companies located in the same state or province in which the prospective employer operates can tell you the year your prospective employer's company became a proprietorship, partnership, or limited company. Although this may not be the year the company actually became a legal entity, it would still give you a reasonably good indication of how long the firm has been operating.

3. Do you think the employer will actually expect more work from you than the job description you read says?

You could find after you start a job that the employer misrepresented the nature of the work, the wages to be paid or the conditions of employment. Unless you are prepared to accept whatever comes, you should clarify as much as possible with the employer what will be expected of you and be sure that is what you are willing to do.

4. Are the policies and procedures of this firm clearly established in writing?

If they are not, you may occasionally find yourself being taken advantage of by fellow employees who are supposed to be "in the know" about such matters.

Sometimes the larger companies have a policies and procedures manual that is made available to employees upon request. When this is the case, you can read for yourself in black and white exactly what services and/or products the company provides to the community and how these services are to be administered.

5. What kinds of tasks will you be expected to do infrequently?

Let's say you were hired by an organization to set up community programs for senior citizens. This type of work may sound interesting, but what if you discover later that you are also responsible for scrubbing down the floors where programs have been staged. This job duty may come as a very unpleasant surprise. Therefore, find out from the prospective employer (during the job interview) what you are expected to do infrequently.

6. What tasks will occupy the main portion of your time?

This question would be of particular interest if you are accepting a position that you are totally unfamiliar with. For example, if you were considering a job as a tax inspector, you want might to know if you'll be out in the community making client calls most of the day or in an office spending most of your time reading narrative and statistical reports. The answer to a question like this could be the deciding factor on whether or not you'll accept the job.

7. How many hours of work per week will you be expected to put in?

Arctic employment sometimes involves working 12 hours per day seven days a week. This is how the big wages are earned. Is the job you are applying for one of those in which an unusually high amount of overtime is required? If so, how much time can you afford to be away from your family in an average work day?

8. How high is the cost of living in the area you will be working in?

If you found a job in an isolated area, the salary may look attractive but how much do you have to spend on food, rent, clothing, and entertainment (if there is any) not to mention the occasional trips you might take to get away from it all. Other points that you should think about before deciding to move to an isolated area are:

- the availability of living accommodations,

- emergency medical care facilities, and

- recreational resources for your family.

9. Will you be expected to progress through higher levels too rapidly?

"Not a chance," you may be saying to yourself. But sometimes (especially in large companies) employees are pushed from one level to another before they have had sufficient time to learn their first job. The result of being pushed too fast is that the employee becomes less and less competent at the job and more and more frustrated. So find out during the job interview the expected rate (or timetable) of progression.

10. Will your personal contributions and achievements get the kind of recognition they deserve?

The quality and quantity of work you do for an employer may be well above average. But if the employer fails to see how productive you are, your efforts could be all in vain.

11. Are you allowed to apply for new openings within the firm for which you qualify or will outside people be considered first?

As time goes on, you may desire opportunities for more personal growth and self-development. However, when new job openings occur within the company, you may be surprised to learn that they will be advertised externally, and not internally. How come? Company policy. So find out from the prospective employer what the company's policy is on this matter.

12. Will there be meaningful communication between you and fellow workers?

If every time you have a problem with a coworker, you have to go running to whoever is in charge to resolve it, you are experiencing problems in communication. Ask the prospective employer during the job interview about the staff's ability to communicate purposefully with each other. Even if the answer to this question is unsatisfactory, you will have at least expressed your concern for meaningful dialogue.

13. Do you feel you can be highly successful at this job?

The job you are applying for could be too complicated for you or too simple. In either case, you may have a difficult time performing at the expected level. Usually the best jobs are those that make you reach out a little beyond what you normally do. These jobs make the very best use of your skills and abilities, but allow you enough room to learn new things.

14. Will this job only let you scratch the surface of your intellectual and creative potential?

You could end up bored to tears with the kind of work you are applying for. Are you sure there are enough interesting aspects of this job to make it challenging? If not, you may frequently find yourself trying to appear busy or contemplating leaving the company when the first available opportunity arises.

15. Does the prospective employer impress you as someone who would be sensitive to your needs?

Sure it is a subjective question. But your personal observations of the person who will be paying your salary must count for something. Was this person helpful to you in answering your questions during the job interview? If the answers were short and evasive, perhaps he or she will be the same on job related problems.

16. Does the prospective employer seem patient and understanding?

What if you are incompatible with another employee in the same firm? And what if your incompatibility stems from the fact that you do not always see eye-to-eye on job related problems? Who is going to resolve your differences of opinion? All your complaints about a fellow employee may be completely justified, but if the boss refuses to get involved in a constructive way, you might as well pack now for the trip down the road. Because by the time this kind of employer does get involved, it's only to scream at you, "You're fired!"

15

THE PROBATIONARY PERIOD: NOW THAT YOU HAVE THE JOB, CAN YOU KEEP IT?

a. EMPLOYEE EVALUATION

One of the biggest problems you face after being hired is that many employers have an inadequate method (if any method at all) for assessing and measuring your overall contribution to their business.

In assessing your productivity, employers are most apt to rely heavily upon their own personal feelings and observations. Or worse, they will go by the subjective comments of those who are assigned the task of staff performance appraisal — supervisors. In either case, your valuable contributions towards creating a smooth running organization may not get the recognition they deserve.

Have a look at the Staff Performance Appraisal Form in Sample #16. This appraisal form is a representative sample of what many employers go by when assessing the performance of their employees. What is interesting about it is this: most of the questions appraisers are asked to answer are ones where only a personal opinion would be given. Question "E" for instance, "What do you consider the employee's strongest job related points?" might be answered by an appraiser in this way: "Independence, solid job knowledge and organization." But this is just an opinion. Another appraiser assessing the same person might say "fairly" well organized. All of these words are relative. They are all open to interpretation. This means that for the person being appraised a lot depends upon the objectivity and intelligence of the appraiser.

As a matter of fact, performance evaluation forms can be very misleading even when the appraiser is objective and intelligent. For example, what if the appraiser says the employee's strongest points are "independence, solid job knowledge and organization" but for the question, "What do you consider the employee's weakest points?" the appraiser enters "attendance." What do all the previous complimentary words mean now? Not much — right? Yet no one really knows how bad the employee's attendance is. It's not quantified. The employee may have only missed four half days out of the entire year. However, the question asked of the appraiser is not how many days has the employee missed in the last year, but what do you consider to be the employee's weakest points.

So you can see that performance appraisal forms can contain more of the prejudices and biases of the appraiser than reliable information about how well the employee is actually doing.

The best that you can do as an employee to protect yourself against an undeserving appraisal is the following.

First of all, make sure you know what your job description says. The job description spells out what the main areas of responsibility are for the job you have been hired to do. Your ability to perform competently on the job has a strong relationship to what you perceive your responsibilities to be. Therefore, get the correct definition of your duties at the outset.

SAMPLE #16
STAFF PERFORMANCE APPRAISAL FORM

NAME OF EMPLOYEE:_____

DEPARTMENT:_____

JOB CLASSIFICATION:_____

APPRAISER'S NAME:_____

CODE: N/A — NOT APPLICABLE; A — ABOVE AVERAGE; N — NORMAL;
B — BELOW AVERAGE; U — UNACCEPTABLE

	N/A	A	N	B	U
1. OVERALL QUALITY OF WORK					
Technical information bearing on job					
Organizing and planning ability					
Thoroughness and accuracy of work completed					
Ability to carry out instructions					
2. OVERALL QUANTITY OF WORK					
Ability to handle various stresses and strains					
Amount of work completed					
Desire for challenging tasks					
3. ATTITUDE TOWARDS JOB					
4. CO-OPERATIVENESS WITH FELLOW WORKERS AND SUPERVISOR					
5. SPEED IN LEARNING NEW RESPONSIBILITIES					
6. PERSONAL APPEARANCE					
7. ATTENDANCE RECORD					
8. PUNCTUALITY					
9. ABILITY TO COMMUNICATE WITH STAFF AND CLIENTS					
Orally					
In writing					
10. DEPENDABILITY					
11. JUDGEMENT					
12. SUPERVISORY CAPACITY					
Skill in promoting co-operation among workers					
Ability in promoting high performance standards					
Interpersonal communication skills					
Performance evaluation skills					
Skill in providing basic training to staff					
Ability in interpreting policies and procedures					
Desire for professional growth & self-development					

APPRAISER'S COMMENTS

_____

A. Have there been any unusual difficulties or problems for you in dealing with the employee?

_____YES/NO

B. In your personal estimation are you happy with the overall performance of the employee

_____YES/NO

C. Does the employee understand the job's dimensions?   _____YES/NO

D. Is the employee currently undergoing any special training program to help him/her more adequately fulfill the specifications of this position?   _____YES/NO

E. What do you consider the employee's strongest job related points?_____

_____

F. What do you consider the employee's weakest points?_____

_____

G. For what period of time have you been overseeing the employee's activities?_____

_____

H. Do you recommend that the employee should:

    1. Be on a probationary period for a while longer   _____YES/NO

    2. Be accepted as a full-time employee   _____YES/NO

    3. Be promoted   _____YES/NO

    4. Be terminated   _____YES/NO

    5. Other _____

ADDITIONAL REMARKS:

_____

_____

_____

APPRAISER'S SIGNATURE:_____

TO THE EMPLOYEE BEING EVALUATED:

Having read and fully understood the above evaluation of your work experience, do you:

1. Agree that it is a fair and accurate reflection of you?   _____YES/NO

2. Challenge the authenticity and reasonableness of the appraiser's rating?   _____YES/NO

EMPLOYEE'S COMMENTS:

_____

_____

_____

DATE: _____

Second, spend some time writing out what you consider to be your major and minor duties. (The job description never says it all — it just provides the main highlights.) Then keep track of how much time you spend doing each task. By doing this, you will not only become more intimately aware of your total range of responsibilities, you will also:

(a) Be able to determine how much time you are giving to activities that really count in helping the company achieve its principal goals, and

(b) Be able to see whether or not your energies should be concentrated on more important job related matters.

Third, keep a list of all your more important accomplishments for the company. No one else will do this for you. And if the prospect of promotion presents itself to you in the future, you will have more proof on your resume of your suitability.

Fourth, secure the job descriptions of all those employees you have regular contact with. By being aware of what other employees are expected to do, you will be helping yourself establish more purposeful communication with them on job related problems.

In going through all of the above mentioned steps, you will be gathering written proof to supply an employer with should you ever need to challenge a supervisor's appraisal of you.

Furthermore, if you do get dismissed from your job due to the results of an unfair appraisal, you will have some evidence to offer the people at the Employment Standards Branch (see sections **b.** and **c.**) as to why you consider your dismissal unjust. Remember this: your complaint about an unjustifiable dismissal to the Employment Standards Branch will be decided upon the basis of your evidence against the employer's.

If you get consistently good evaluations from your supervisor and it looks as though you can keep your job, there is only one more thing left for you to do: know your rights under your state or provincial employment act.

There are minimum standards that employers must adhere to in their relationship to employees. You can find out what these standards are by writing to the Employment Standards Branch in your area. For questions about discrimination, check with the Civil/Human Rights Commission near you (see sections **d.** and **e.**). Here is a list of some of the more important questions you should have answers to:

(a) Can my employer rightfully pay me in any time period he or she decides to (i.e., every third or fourth week instead of every week or second week)?

(b) Does an employer have to give me a statement of my wages when I am paid?

(c) Is there a minimum wage that I should be receiving for this job?

(d) If I work more than eight hours per day or forty hours per week am I entitled to time and one-half my regular rate of pay?

(e) What can I do about an employer who owes wages and refuses to pay?

(f) Do I have to work more than eight hours per day for an employer?

(g) What general holidays am I entitled to each year? How many days do I first have to work before being eligible for these holidays?

(h) How many weeks of vacation pay am I entitled to each year?

(i) Am I entitled to time off the job to vote in state/federal or provincial elections?

(j) Am I entitled to maternity leave of absence during or after pregnancy?

81

(k) I've just been fired. What reasons are justifiable? What action can I proceed with if the reasons are not justifiable?

(l) Am I entitled to severance pay if I have been dismissed without being given sufficient notice?

(m) Can an employer make deductions from my pay check (i.e., union dues, insurance premiums, charitable donations, savings plans, pension plan, etc.) without first getting my permission?

For help in Canada in getting the answers to these and other legal questions, see your provincial edition of *Employee/Employer Rights,* another title in the Self-Counsel Series.

b. UNITED STATES: EMPLOYMENT STANDARDS ADMINISTRATION

Employment Standards Administration
200 Constitution Avenue N.W.
Washington, D.C. 20210
Telephone: (202) 523-8743

c. CANADA: LABOUR CANADA EMPLOYMENT STANDARDS BRANCH

FEDERAL
Employment Standards & Equal Pay
Labour Canada
Place du Portage, Phase II
Ottawa, ON
K1A 0J2
(819) 997-1645

BRITISH COLUMBIA
Employment Standards Branch
Department of Labour
Parliament Buildings
Victoria, BC
V8V 1X4
(604) 387-1220

ALBERTA
Employment Standards Branch
Alberta Labour
4th Floor
10339 – 124th Street
Edmonton, AB
T5N 3W1
(403) 427-8541

SASKATCHEWAN
Employment Standards Division
Department of Labour
1870 Albert Street
Regina, SK
S4P 3V7
(306) 787-2474

MANITOBA
Employment Standards Division
Department of Labour & Employment Services
607 Norquay Building
401 York Avenue
Winnipeg, MB
R3C 0P8
(204) 945-3352

ONTARIO
Employment Standards Branch
Ministry of Labour
40 Dundas Street West
Tower 'B'
4th Floor
Toronto, ON
M5G 2C2
(416) 326-7000

QUEBEC
Directeur du Service de Decrets
425 rue St. Amable
Ministere du Travail
Quebec, PQ
G1R 4Z1
(418) 643-4415

NEW BRUNSWICK
Employment Standards Branch
Department of Labour
P.O. Box 6000
470 York Street
2nd Floor, Room 203
Fredericton, NB
E3B 5H1
(506) 453-2725

NOVA SCOTIA
Labour Standards Division
Department of Labour & Manpower
Box 697
Halifax, NS
B3J 2T8
(902) 424-4311

PRINCE EDWARD ISLAND
Employment Standards Advisory Board
Department of Labour
Box 2000
Charlottetown, PE
C1A 7N8
(902) 368-5550

NEWFOUNDLAND
Director of Labour Standards
Department of Labour & Manpower
Confederation Building
St. John's, NF
A1C 5T7
(709) 576-2742

YUKON
Co-ordinator of Labour Services
Consumer, Corporate & Labour Affairs
Branch
Department of Justice
P.O. Box 2703
Whitehorse, YT
Y1A 2C6
(403) 667-5312

d. UNITED STATES: CIVIL RIGHTS COMMISSION

Complaints Referral
American Commission On Civil Rights
1121 Vermont Avenue N.W.
Washington, D.C. 20425
Toll Free: 1-800-552-6843
Telephone:(202) 376-8513

e. CANADA: HUMAN RIGHTS COMMISSION

FEDERAL
Canadian Human Rights Commission
320 Queen Street
13th Floor
Place de Ville
Tower 'A'
Ottawa, ON
K1A 1E1
(613) 995-1151
(613) 426-2687 (fax)
1-800-565-1752 (toll free)

BRITISH COLUMBIA
British Columbia Human Rights
Commission
Parliament Buildings
Victoria, BC
V8V 1X4
(604) 387-3710
(604) 387-3643 (fax)
1-800-742-6117 (toll free)

ALBERTA
Alberta Human Rights Commission
902 — 10808 — 99th Avenue
Edmonton, AB
T5K 0G5
(403) 427-3116
(403) 422-3563 (fax)

SASKATCHEWAN
Saskatchewan Human Rights Commission
8th Floor, Cantebury Towers
224 — 4th Avenue S.
Saskatoon, SK
S7K 2H6
(306) 933-5952
(306) 933-7863 (fax)

MANITOBA
Manitoba Human Rights Commission
Paris Building
Room 301
259 Portage Avenue
Winnipeg, MB
R3B 2A9
(204) 945-3007
(204) 945-1292 (fax)

NORTHWEST TERRITORIES
Senior Labour Officer
Labour Division
Government of the N.W.T.
P.O. Box 1320
Yellowknife, NT
X1A 2L9
(403) 902-3359
(403) 873-0260 (fax)

ONTARIO
Ontario Human Rights Commission
400 University Avenue
Toronto, ON
M7A 2R9
(416) 965-6841
(416) 965-3197 (fax)

QUEBEC
Commission des droits de la Personne
360 — rue St. Jacques
Montreal, PQ
H2Y 1P5
(514) 873-5146
(514) 873-6032 (fax)

NEW BRUNSWICK
New Brunswick Human Rights
Commission
P.O. Box 6000
103 Church Street
Fredericton, NB
E3B 5H1
(506) 453-2301
(506) 453-2653 (fax)

NOVA SCOTIA
Nova Scotia Human Rights Commission
P.O. Box 2221
Halifax, NS
B3J 3C4
(902) 424-4111
(902) 424-0550 (fax)

PRINCE EDWARD ISLAND
P.E.I. Human Rights Commission
Box 2000
Charlottetown, PE
C1A 7N8
(902) 368-4180
(902) 368-4326 (fax)

NEWFOUNDLAND
Newfoundland Human Rights
Commission
Department of Justice
P.O. Box 8700
345 Duckworth Street
6th Floor
St. John's, NF
A1B 4J6
(709) 576-2709
(709) 576-0790 (fax)

16
COMMUNITY RESOURCES:
WHO IS HELPING WHOM OUT THERE?

a. THE BUREAU OF CORPORATIONS AND/OR COMPANY REGISTRAR OFFICE

Your most valuable source of help when looking for work is the Bureau of Corporations (in the United States) and the Registrar of Companies (in Canada) discussed in chapter 10.

These offices are most valuable because through them you can obtain the names and addresses of people with hiring power in the company you would like to work for, as well as important information on the nature of their services and/or products, size, length of time in business, etc. You have purposeful communication about yourself in writing (i.e., your resume) and now it is simply a question of getting the key people in those companies you want to work for to read about you. So rely very heavily upon the Bureau of Corporations or company registrar's office for determining who those people are. Then check the sources discussed below.

b. NEWSPAPER ADVERTISEMENTS

Obviously newspaper ads can be a valuable source of information on job opportunities. Just remember to thoroughly check out those companies that interest you through the Bureau of Corporations and/or Registrar of Companies before sending them your resume.

c. ARE PRIVATE EMPLOYMENT AGENCIES ANY GOOD FOR JOB HUNTERS?

Perhaps, but do not expect too much from private employment agencies in general, because they usually specialize in particular kinds of jobs or a particular industry. For example, some agencies only see people with technical backgrounds; others look for the professional or managerial types; some specialize in finding stenographic and clerical personnel for businesses; others look for administrative people. Thus, whether an employment agency can help you depends on their speciality and your background.

Also keep in mind that in the United States, private employment agencies (also known as head hunters, executive search firms, and management consultants), can charge job hunters for their services, and might ask you to sign a contract before representing you. Because of this, "Let the buyer beware!" If you intend to employ their services, you should first run a thorough check on them through the Bureau of Corporations to find out the year in which they were first established. It is common knowledge that many private employment agencies go in and out of business regularly; and one test, perhaps, for determining their reliability and honesty in dealing with their clients, is the number of years they have been in existence.

In Canada the services of private employment agencies are provided to the job hunter free of charge.

d. WHAT ABOUT PUBLIC EMPLOYMENT AGENCIES?

You probably already know about USES (United States Employment Service). It is a Federal State employment system. Employers use the services of USES for screening their job applicants mainly because they are free. (Private employment agencies bill employers for their services because they conduct a thorough background check on candidates that they refer to businesses.)

In Canada, Employment & Immigration Canada provides a service to employers and job hunters that is similar to USES. Employers use Employment & Immigration Canada mainly because it is a federally funded employment agency providing screening services free of charge.

The people who can best take advantage of the job information services provided by public employment centers are those who are entering the job market for the first time and "blue-collar" workers.

e. THE CHAMBER OF COMMERCE

The Chamber of Commerce is an association primarily for business people. I say primarily because you or anyone can become a member (by paying an annual membership fee), but it is primarily the business person who joins. As a member of the Chamber of Commerce, a business person gets a certain amount of free promotion of goods and services.

There are two advantages for the job hunter in contacting the Chamber of Commerce.

(a) The Chamber of Commerce can provide you with literature on a particular community that you might consider moving to. For example, if you live in Olympia, Washington, and are considering relocation to Tallahassee, Florida, then you would write to the Chamber in Tallahassee requesting their literature on this city. The Chamber would forward to you (whether you are a member or not) a pamphlet describing the city of Tallahassee (i.e., major industries, population, community resources, etc.) showing you pictures of various parts of the city and state. (You can find out the addresses of any Chamber by contacting your local Chamber of Commerce and asking them to provide you with the addresses you want).

(b) Each Chamber of Commerce publishes an annual roster that contains the names and telephone numbers of all its members. You can have a roster by becoming a member. With that roster, you have another method of identifying people with hiring power in the community you wish to work in.

f. CANADA: JOBS IN GOVERNMENT, TRANSPORTATION, UNIVERSITIES, OR FINANCIAL INSTITUTIONS

Go to the public library and ask for the *Canadian Almanac and Directory*, published annually by Copp Clark Company Limited, Toronto. This reference book (i.e., it can't be taken home from the library) lists government departments and addresses at federal, provincial, and municipal levels as well as their chief officials, addresses and telephone numbers.

The *Canadian Almanac and Directory* provides the names of directors of hospitals, libraries, colleges, universities, banks, insurance and trust companies throughout Canada. It contains a comprehensive list of Canadian cities, towns, and villages and gives you their population.

g. FOR CANADIANS CONSIDERING A MOVE TO THE UNITED STATES

Go to the public library and ask for *Standard & Poor's Registrar of Corporations, Directors and Executives*, published annually by Standard & Poor's Corporation, New York.

In this directory you will find the names, addresses and telephone numbers of 55,000 corporations, with information on the names, titles, and functions of their directors, officers, and other principals, the names of their accounting firms, primary bank and law firm, their primary products and/or services, and addresses of their executives. (If you are not sure how to use reference books like this one and the one mentioned above, ask the librarian for assistance; and don't feel you are inconveniencing them by doing so; their job is to assist you.)

● ● ●

Now it's time to test the techniques of job hunting offered to you in this book. You have everything you need to clearly demonstrate your employable value to employers — a professional-looking resume and covering letter. You have a good indication of how your competition summarizes their work related strengths on the resume.

You know how to research companies of interest to you and how to ensure that no one except the employer in person will be assessing your potential as an employee. And when you finally go to the job interview, you know what kind of questions to expect and how to answer them.

You have a valuable marketing plan for finding and securing meaningful employment. The only thing to do now is use it to your best advantage.

APPENDIX
SAMPLE RESUMES

RESUME #1
APPRAISER

Betty C. Lander
22 Bullion Avenue
Edmonton, Alberta
T5J 3A3

Home telephone: (403) 427-1111

PERSONAL INFORMATION

Birth date: October 19, 1963

Marital status: married   Dependents: none

EDUCATIONAL BACKGROUND

Property Appraisals: Edmonton Community College, Edmonton, Alberta, 1983 - 1985
  Civil Engineering Technology Program: Edmonton Community College, Edmonton,
  Alberta, 1981 - 1983

Diploma (Grade 12 Academic): Cormier Senior High School, Edmonton, Alberta,
  1981

PROFESSIONAL DESIGNATIONS

AACI Designation, granted through the Appraisal Institute of Canada, May 1991

Canadian Residential Appraiser (CRA), granted through the Appraisal Institute
  of Canada, May 1988

PROFESSIONAL AFFILIATIONS

Member in good standing of the Appraisal Institute of Canada since 1983

Member in good standing of the Alberta Provincial Chapter of the Appraisal
  Institute of Canada since 1983

SPECIAL SKILLS AND ABILITIES

- Possess strong interpersonal communication skills, and have a demonstrated
  interest in working harmoniously with others
- Have a strong knowledge of building technology standards and specifications, drafting, carpentry, and joinery

PROFESSIONAL INTERESTS: reading the CANADIAN APPRAISER MAGAZINE

AVAILABILITY: Minimum of two weeks' notice required.

PROFESSIONAL EXPERIENCE

June 1985 - present: full-time employment

        The Appraisals Ltd.
        96 Real Estate Avenue
        Edmonton, Alberta

Real Estate Appraiser for this company which specializes in the provision of comprehensive real estate appraisal and consulting services for financial institutions, municipal, provincial and federal government departments, insurance companies, oil companies, utility companies, real estate development companies, large manufacturing companies, large retail and service chains, insurance claim adjustment companies, and the general public.

TYPES OF PROPERTIES PERSONALLY APPRAISED: Land; Single and Multiple Family Residences; Condominiums; Sub-Divisions; Commercial, Agricultural, Industrial, and Institutional properties.

TYPES OF APPRAISAL ASSIGNMENTS PERSONALLY COMPLETED: Loan Appraisals; Expropriation Appraisals; Tax Assessment Appraisals; Estate Settlement Appraisals; Marketability and Highest and Best Use Studies; Investment Analysis and Counselling; Review of Appraisals; Appraisals for Tax Purposes (Capital Gains).

Specific duties involve conducting property appraisals that take into consideration the following: gathering and analyzing all pertinent information on property appraisals (i.e., sales data, rental information, construction cost, etc.); interpreting property maps, technical specifi-cations and blueprints; gathering specific data on properties to be appraised; conducting inspections of properties; formulating value estimates based on the analysis of data gathered; preparing appraisal reports which contain recommendations and summaries of findings.

BUSINESS REFERENCES
Mr. Tom Prop, President
The Appraisals Ltd.
96 Real Estate Avenue
Edmonton, Alberta
T5J 3A3
Business telephone: (403) 427-0000

Mr. John Doe, Regional Director of Assessments
Department of Municipal Affairs
(Regional Assessment Office)
Edmonton, Alberta
Business telephone: (403) 427-2222

RESUME #2
AUTOMOTIVE MECHANIC

Alan B. Mechanna
123 Repair Drive
Montgomery, AL 36130

Home telephone: (205) 242-1111

PERSONAL INFORMATION

Birth date: September 23, 1953
Health: excellent

EDUCATIONAL BACKGROUND

Certificate of Qualification in Motor Vehicle Repair: Montgomery Institute
   of Trades, Montgomery, Alabama, 1973

Diploma: Carmel Public School, Montgomery, Alabama, 1971

EMERGENCY FIRST AID CERTIFICATE

Safety Oriented First Aid, taken through the St. John Ambulance, Montgomery, Alabama, currently valid

AVAILABILITY: Minimum of two weeks' notice required.

PROFESSIONAL EXPERIENCE

September 1973 - present: full-time employment

   American Tire Inc.
   73 Fixit Drive
   Montgomery, Alabama

Automotive Technician/Mechanic for this company which specializes in automotive
   and light truck mechanical repairs. Principal duties and responsibilities involve the following:

MECHANICAL/ELECTRICAL REPAIRS: Responsible for conducting tests to determine
   the reliability and power capacity of engines; serving as a troubleshooter
   to diagnose and repair complex mechanical and electrical malfunctions (i.e.,
   overhauling and rebuilding engines; repairing electronic fuel injections;
   shock replacements; damage repairs to cooling systems; metal replacements;
   restoration work; doing tune-ups and wheel balancing, etc.); setting up en-
   gine governors; putting in turbo blowers; observing good housekeeping standards in order to ensure the occupational health and safety of fellow workers; ongoing inspection of the quality of personal work completed, in order
   to ensure conformance to requirements, technical excellence, and adherence
   to sound professional practices.

BUSINESS REFERENCES: Available Upon Request.

BANK MANAGER

Joseph P. Overseer
503 Fundy Court
Toronto, Ontario
M7A 2H6

Home telephone: (416) 596-1111

PERSONAL INFORMATION

Birth date: March 8, 1959
Marital status: married

EDUCATIONAL BACKGROUND

Fellowship of the Institute of Canadian Bankers (F.I.C.B.), sponsored by The Big Bank of Canada, 1985 – 1988

Bachelor of Business Administration: University of Ottawa, Ottawa, Ontario, 1981

Diploma (Grade 12 Academic): Roland High School, Ottawa, Ontario, 1977

SPECIAL SKILLS AND ABILITIES

- Possess strong interpersonal communication skills, and have a demonstrated interest in working harmoniously with others

- Have strong organizing, managing, and motivating skills

BUSINESS EXPERIENCE

June 1981 – present

The Big Bank of Canada
125 University Avenue
Toronto, Ontario

Branch Manager (Present Job Title)
[Promoted from the position of **Manager Trainee**, working at branch operations in Trenton, Ontario (June 1981 – March 1982) to **Accountant**, working at branch operations in Ottawa, Ontario (March 1982 – June 1984) to **Credit Officer**, working at branch operations in Toronto, Ontario (June 1984 – May 1986) to **Assistant Manager**, working at branch operations in Oshawa, Ontario (May 1986 – April 1988) to **Branch Manager** of the Toronto, Ontario operation (April 1988 – present)]
Reporting directly to the District Manager on business objectives and results, principal duties and responsibilities involve the following:
Staff Supervision: Responsible for the direct supervision of the Assistant Bank Manager, Accountant and Secretary, and for the indirect supervision of twenty-nine subordinates (e.g., planning and scheduling of workloads; assigning tasks; establishing priorities; promoting a team approach in the implementation and management of the bank's goals, objectives and processes);
Bringing In New Business Accounts: Responsible for formulating sales strategy and direction in order to bring in new retail accounts for the bank (e.g., market development, major account sales activities, etc.); drafting and presenting proposals which emphasize the selling points and benefits of the bank's business and financial

services to prospective clients; evaluating finance plans, as well as keeping abreast of market trends, business cycles, and economic indicators;

Approving Personal & Commercial Loans & Mortgages: Responsible for evaluating the financial needs of clients and researching into available finance opportunities; verifying the ability and determining the willingness of potential clients to pay back borrowed funds (e.g., analyzing the financial statements of prospective clients; conducting credit checks and personal interviews); approving loans and mortgages; collecting on past due accounts, when required);

Budget Administration: Responsible for ensuring that all financial transactions pertaining to the bank's budget are properly administered and authorized and in accordance with established policies; authorizing cash payments; controlling, developing and evaluating all phases of financial reporting;

Organizing & Implementing Sales Training Programs: Responsible for organizing, implementing and instructing in Sales Training Programs for all of the bank's employees, which deal with product knowledge and proper sales techniques of Registered Retirement Savings Plans, Guaranteed Investment Certificates, Credit Cards, and other financial products;

Personnel Administration: Responsible for scheduling and conducting job interviews with prospective employees; preparing financial forecasts on the short and long term personnel requirements of the bank; counselling employees experiencing problems which may be affecting their on-the-job performance, in order to facilitate their return to optimal efficiency (e.g. stresses and strains engendered by working conditions or incompatibility with fellow workers); conducting Employee Performance & Potential Evaluations.

BUSINESS & CHARACTER REFERENCES:

Available upon request.

BANK TELLER

Charlene H. Cheque
128 Fernwood Avenue, Apt. 4
Regina, Saskatchewan
S4P 3V7

Home telephone: (306) 565-0000

PERSONAL INFORMATION

Birth date: December 23, 1953
Marital status: single   Dependents: none
Health: excellent

EDUCATIONAL BACKGROUND

Diploma (Grade 12 Academic): Regina Senior High School, Regina, Saskatchewan, 1971

SPECIAL SKILLS AND ABILITIES

- Possess strong interpersonal communication skills, and have a demonstrated interest in working harmoniously with others
- Can present a professional company image to clients, fellow workers, subordinates and/or peers

RELOCATE: Willing to relocate.

HOBBIES AND INTERESTS: meeting people; reading literature; physical fitness

(i.e., jogging, downhill skiing, walking); sports in general

BANKING EXPERIENCE

October 1985 – January 1991: full-time employment
Mutual Bank of Saskatchewan
671 Main Street
Regina, Saskatchewan

Teller

Reporting directly to the Head Teller, principal duties and responsibilities involved the following:

BANKING DUTIES: Responsible for maintaining business and personal chequing/savings accounts
(e.g., monthly chequing account changes; processing payments on credit cards; transfer of funds to savings and/or chequing accounts; withdrawals and deposits; calculation and entry of dividends); preparing and mailing monthly statements; reconciliation of cash on hand; computer posting; daily balancing and posting of clearing; calculating monthly interest payments on loans and savings accounts; preparing and mailing monthly billing statements; making calculations on foreign exchange currencies for individuals and corporations; strictly adhering to the bank's policies on all confidential matters; acquiring a working knowledge of the general operating procedures of other departments and divisions within the bank;

CUSTOMER RELATIONS: Responsible for handling the inquiries and/or complaints of customers in a polite and professional manner; selling Guaranteed Investment Certificates, Registered Retirement Savings Plans, Credit Cards and other financial products, as well as explaining payment schedules; promoting public awareness of the bank's financial services through good customer service.

October 1983 – October 1985: full-time employment
        Green Cross of Canada
        123 MacBeath Avenue
        Regina, Saskatchewan

<u>Data Entry Clerk</u>

June 1971 – October 1983: full-time employment
        Ben's Drug Mart
        Royalty Mall
        Regina, Saskatchewan

<u>Cashier</u>

<u>BUSINESS REFERENCES</u>

Mr. Albert Comeau, Manager
Mutual Bank of Saskatchewan
671 Main Street
Regina, Saskatchewan
S4P 3V7
Business telephone (306) 565-1111

<u>ADDITIONAL REMARKS</u>: I am a results-oriented individual, and can work profitably, independently, or in cooperation with others; and I work with enthusiasm and high energy on all assignments.

RESUME #5
BARTENDER

Roy B. Tender
123 Bamford Road
Phoenix, AZ 85007

Home telephone: (602) 542-2222

PERSONAL INFORMATION

Birth date: June 1, 1961
Height: 5' 11"   Weight: 175 lbs.
Health: excellent

EDUCATIONAL BACKGROUND

Diploma: Birchmount High School, Phoenix, Arizona, 1979

BARTENDING CERTIFICATE

Certificate of Bartending, taken through the Comprehensive School of Bartending, Phoenix, Arizona, 1979

HOBBIES AND INTERESTS: meeting people; physical fitness; wine appreciation

AVAILABILITY: Minimum of two weeks' notice required.

BARTENDING EXPERIENCE

September 1979 - present: full-time employment

>   Drink & Dine Night Club
>   123 Bottle Drive
>   Phoenix, Arizona

Bartender for this licensed entertainment center. Reporting directly to the Owner on business objectives and results, principal duties and responsibilities involve the following:

PUBLIC RELATIONS: Responsible for receiving customer payments in cash and/or credit card; handling the inquiries and/or complaints of clients in a polite and professional manner; preparing customer drinks; promoting public awareness of the club through good customer service;

IN-HOUSE DEPOSITS: Responsible for making daily in-house deposits of amounts as high as $5,000.00; balancing receipts, as well as forwarding a record of such receipts to the Accounting Department;

INVENTORY CONTROL: Responsible for ordering, issuing and controlling inventory on all alcohol products and mixes for the bar; pricing drinks.

BUSINESS REFERENCES: Available Upon Request.

Angela J. Profit
78 Ledger Road
Toronto, Ontario
M7A 2H6

Home telephone: (506) 382-4136

PERSONAL INFORMATION

Birth date: February 26, 1953
Marital status: single   .
Height: 5' 3"   Weight: 140 lbs.
Health: excellent

EDUCATIONAL BACKGROUND

Bookkeeping/Accounting Program: Ontario Institute of Technology (Toronto Campus), Toronto, Ontario, 1973
Diploma (Grade 12 Academic): Harrison Senior High School, Toronto, Ontario, 1971

COMPANY SPONSORED ACCOUNTING COURSE COMPLETED

Lotus 1-2-3 (Computer Spread Sheets & Graphics): sponsored by Architectural
  Construction Ltd. (in-house training), Toronto, Ontario, 1989

SPECIAL TRAINING: Willing to undergo any amount of special training deemed
  necessary to more adequately meet the continuing demands of this position.

BONDABLE: I am bondable, and can pass a police security check.

SALARY EXPECTED: Open — nature and challenge of position itself is of principal concern.

BUSINESS EXPERIENCE

May 1974 - January 1991: full-time employment

  Architectural Construction Ltd.
  131 Balsam Avenue
  Toronto, Ontario

Bookkeeper for this architectural contracting company.
Reporting directly to the President and Vice President on business objectives and results, principal duties and responsibilities involved the following:

General Accounting: Responsible for controlling, developing and evaluating
all phases of financial reporting (i.e., preparation of financial statements; reporting on compliance for government grants; etc.); handling all
accounting functions related to sales and inventory distribution (i.e., inventory reconciliation; subledger maintenance and balancing; journal entry
preparation, etc.); preparing pro forma financial statements; acting as a liaison between the company and key customer accounts on matters pertaining to
fiscal responsibility;

Bookkeeping: Responsible for maintaining computerized accounting ledgers (i.e., accounts payable/receivable; preparing profit and loss statements and other financial statements); maintaining all accounting records under a double entry ledger system (i.e., sales, cash receipts, and cash disbursing); assisting the Chartered Accountant on accounting, financial and operating procedure audits; handling inventory control for cost of sales; making daily bank deposits and preparing cash and credit card reconciliations on amounts as high as $210,000;

Managing Payroll Procedures: Responsible for managing the payroll procedures for full and part-time employees; verifying daily time sheets of employees; calculating salary deductions affecting Income Tax, Canada Pension Plan, Unemployment Insurance Commission, Union Dues, Auxiliary Allowance, Superannuation and/or required hours for auxiliary benefit package; retro pay calculations; recovering outstanding advances; calculating holiday pay and pay advances for holiday purposes; preparing records of employment regarding the Unemployment Insurance Commission; maintaining all accounting files; preparing, calculating and using correct forms for leaves-without-pay, short term injury and illness plan, severance pay, bond payments, and miscellaneous pay vouchers of employees, as required.

TERM POSITION

August 17, 1973 – February 27, 1974: term position

Toronto Food And Clothing Bank
1111 Fare Road
Toronto, Ontario

Bookkeeper for this non-profit community-based organization. Principal duties and responsibilities were similar in nature to the Bookkeeper position with Architectural Construction Ltd., discussed in detail above.

BUSINESS REFERENCES: Available Upon Request.

RESUME #7
CASHIER

Francine R. Cash
84 High Street
Austin, TX 78711

Home telephone: (512) 463-0000

<u>PERSONAL INFORMATION</u>

Marital status: single   Dependents: none
Height: 5' 2"   Weight: 120 lbs.
Health: excellent
Citizenship: American

<u>EDUCATIONAL BACKGROUND</u>

Diploma (Grade 12 Business): Harrison Public High School, Austin, Texas, 1988

<u>WORK EXPERIENCE</u>

October 1988 - present: permanent part-time employment

   The Food Store Ltd.
   234 Mills Road
   Austin, Texas

<u>Cashier</u> for this retail grocery store which is a part of a national chain op-
eration.

Reporting directly to the Store Manager, principal duties and responsibilities involve selling all dry groceries and produce; receiving customer payments in cash and/or personal check; resolving inquiries or complaints from
the general public in a polite and professional manner (i.e., on matters pertaining to sales, lost goods, damages, returns, etc.); planning and scheduling of personal workloads in order to ensure prompt and timely handling of
same; operating an I.B.M. computerized cash register; promoting public awareness of the store through good customer service.

<u>PART-TIME EMPLOYMENT</u> (While Attending School)

September 1984 - October 1988: part-time employment

   Consumers Drugs
   12 Mountain Road
   Austin, Texas

<u>Cashier</u>

<u>BUSINESS REFERENCES</u>: Available Upon Request.

CHARTERED ACCOUNTANT

Lorraine C. Comeau
13 Charter Road
Halifax, Nova Scotia
B3J 2Y4

Home telephone: (902) 424-9999

PERSONAL INFORMATION

Birth date: June 14, 1965
Marital status: single   Dependents: none
Health: excellent

EDUCATIONAL BACKGROUND

Chartered Accountant Designation: Atlantic School of Chartered Accountancy, Halifax, Nova Scotia, 1990

Bachelor of Business Administration: Dalhousie University, Halifax, Nova Scotia, 1987
    Graduated With Distinction

Diploma (Grade 12 Academic): Dartmouth Composite High School, Dartmouth, Nova Scotia, 1983

AWARDS AND SCHOLARSHIPS

Received the 25th Anniversary Business Administration Scholarship in the amount of $800.00 for academic
    studies between 1986 – 1987
Received the Mason Lodge Memorial Scholarship in the amount of $1,500.00 for academic studies between
    1985 – 1986

PROFESSIONAL AFFILIATION

Nova Scotia Association of Chartered Accountants, Halifax, Nova Scotia, member since 1990

KNOWLEDGE OF COMPUTER LANGUAGES
BASIC

KNOWLEDGE OF COMPUTER APPLICATIONS
- Lotus 1-2-3 (Computer Spread Sheets & Graphics)
- Accounting Programs
- Harvard Graphics

PROFESSIONAL INTERESTS: reading C.A. MAGAZINE, THE TAX LETTER, and TAX PROFILE

PROFESSIONAL EXPERIENCE

September 1990 – present: full-time employment
    Ryerson Chartered Accountants
    44 Edifice Hill
    Halifax, Nova Scotia

Senior Audit Assistant, working in the audit department of this international chartered accountant firm.
    <u>Types of Companies/Institutions Personally Audited</u>: a hospital; a large shipping line company; a
    truck transportation company; a frozen food processing company; a wholesaler of industrial
    equipment; a wholesale hardware company; a large law firm; a construction company

    Reporting directly to both the Managers and Partners on business objectives and results, principal
    duties and responsibilities involve the following:

Auditing Existing Accounting Systems Of Clients: Responsible for developing and executing audits on the types of companies mentioned above; using computer assisted audit techniques on the existing accounting systems of clients which control their payroll, accounts receivable/payable, and inventory (i.e., conducting studies of existing computerized reporting systems, methods, and procedures in order to assess the effectiveness of the company's controls; making recommendations in writing to the appropriate representatives of clients on matters pertaining to weaknesses in their control systems; reviewing and documenting systems and related controls);

Taxation: Responsible for preparing and signing Canadian and American corporate tax returns and schedules; providing advice to representatives of the firm's clients on matters pertaining to corporate taxation; ensuring that the firm's clients act in compliance with the Goods & Services Tax Act; maintaining a working knowledge of provincial and federal government income tax acts;

General Accounting: Responsible for controlling, developing and evaluating all phases of financial reporting for the firm's clients (i.e., preparation of financial statements; reporting on compliance for government grants; etc.); handling all accounting functions related to sales and inventory distribution (i.e., inventory reconciliation; subledger maintenance and balancing; journal entry preparation; etc.).

BUSINESS AND CHARACTER REFERENCES: Available Upon Request.

Ronald C. Catalyst
32 Formula Drive
Boise, ID 83720

Home telephone: (208) 334-2300

PERSONAL INFORMATION

Birth date: July 21, 1959
Marital status: single
Health: excellent

EDUCATIONAL BACKGROUND

Chemical Engineering Diploma, University of Idaho, Boise, Idaho, 1984
  B.Sc., University of Idaho, Boise, Idaho, 1982
  Diploma (Grade 12 Academic): Boise Composite High School, Boise, Idaho, 1977

PROFESSIONAL EXPERIENCE

August 1984 - present

  Advanced Scientific Research Ltd.
  123 Concept Avenue
  Boise, Idaho

Analytical Technologist
Reporting to the Chief Chemist, principal duties and responsibilities involve the following:

Conducting Laboratory Tests: Responsible for testing mining and geological samples for precious metals, fluorides, rare earths, beryllium, tungsten, copper, tin, zinc, and free carbon; using computerized instrumentation; overseeing routine process control of plant samples (i.e., extraction of crude gold ingots and ultimate refining into gold bullion);

Research & Development: Responsible for developing new analytical and evaluation procedures in cooperation with other helping professionals; recommending procedures for improving the quality and consistency of products to be marketed to company clients; keeping abreast of the ongoing changes and latest developments in instrumentation and scientific techniques related to the analysis of various types of geological samples.

BUSINESS REFERENCES: Available Upon Request.

RESUME #10
CLERK TYPIST

Henry S. Memo
12 Grafton Street
Boston, MA 02133

Home telephone: (617) 727-1111

PERSONAL INFORMATION

Birth date: March 27, 1961
Marital status: single   Dependents: none
Height: 5' 10"   Weight: 160 lbs.
Health: excellent

EDUCATIONAL BACKGROUND

Secretarial Program: Boston College of Applied Arts & Technology,
   Boston, Massachusetts, 1979 - 1980
Diploma: Colonel Grey Public High School, Boston, Massachusetts, 1979

SPECIAL SKILLS AND ABILITIES

- Can competently operate manual, electric, and computerized typewriters;
   small switchboards; dictating equipment; photocopiers; and calculators

WORK EXPERIENCE

April 1980 - present: full-time employment
        City of Boston
        (Parks/Recreation)
        Boston, Massachusetts

Clerk Typist: Reporting directly to the Office Manager, principal duties and
responsibilities involve typing and composing of letters and memos for signature, with the responsibility for their correct grammar, spelling and punctuation; transcribing and typing minutes of conferences and meetings, memos,
reports, statements, etc. from dictaphone, written notes or verbal instructions; taking dictation; maintaining confidential filing systems to ensure
correct indexing, cross-references, and compliance with office regulations;
personally responsible for updating the Master Files.

BUSINESS REFERENCE

Mrs. Mary Visor, Office Manager
City of Boston
Parks/Recreation)
Boston, Massachusetts
Business telephone: (617) 727-0987

RESUME #11
CONSTRUCTION SUPERINTENDENT

Betty P. Builder
555 Yonge Street
Toronto, Ontario
M7A 2H6
Home telephone: (416) 963-0000

PERSONAL INFORMATION

Birth date: August 3, 1947
Marital status: married   Dependents: four
Height: 5' 8"   Weight: 145 lbs.
Health: excellent

EDUCATIONAL BACKGROUND

Civil Engineering Technology Program: Ontario Community College (Toronto Campus), Toronto, Ontario, 1965 - 1967
Major: Architectural Option
Diploma (Grade 12 Academic): City Centre High School, Toronto, Ontario, 1965

SPECIAL SKILLS AND ABILITIES

- Have a strong knowledge of building technology standards and specifications, drafting, carpentry, and joinery

- Have extensive experience in the preparation of estimates and tenders for major projects

PROFESSIONAL EXPERIENCE

March 1980 - present: full-time employment
  A.B.C. Construction Ltd.
  902 Yonge Street
  Toronto, Ontario

Chief Estimator for this general contracting company which specializes in retail and commercial construction projects (i.e. renovations to existing buildings, interior architectural, mechanical and electrical work, concrete and form work, etc.).
[Largest And Smallest Projects Personally Responsible For (In Terms Of Their Cost And Square Feet) are entered below:

Maximum Cost of Construction:$1.2 Million

Minimum Cost of Construction:$ 40,000.00

Maximum Number of Sq. Ft.:130,000 square feet

Minimum Number of Sq. Ft.: 60,000 square feet
Reporting directly to the President on business objectives and results, principal duties and responsibilities involve the following:

CONCEPTUAL DESIGN WORK & PREPARATION OF ESTIMATES: Responsible for the preparation of conceptual designs (e.g., blueprints and renderings), when required, and preparation of accurate cost data for work order estimates (e.g., material, labour, time requirements, equipment required, etc.); preparing construction plans which ensure completion of work on schedule and within approved budgets;

106

<u>CLIENT RELATIONS</u>: Responsible for working in cooperation with architects, de-
signers and engineers in the planning and execution of projects; discussing
and resolving with municipal and provincial bodies problems related to design, by-laws, codes, municipal planning and organizing, when required; handling inquiries from building and safety inspectors; issuing tenders and contracts; contract administration;

<u>STAFF SUPERVISION</u>: Responsible for supervising the activities of trades and
subtrades people representing the following trades: sitework, formwork & concrete, masonry, structural steel, carpentry & custom millwork, roofing, glaz-
ing, drywall and acoustics, flooring, painting, specialities, plumbing, heat-
ing ventilation and air conditioning, sprinklers and fire protection,
electrical and security systems;

<u>JUST IN TIME/TOTAL QUALITY CONTROL</u>: Responsible for the ongoing inspection
of the quality of work completed by subtrades and trades people in order to
ensure: 1. conformance to requirements; 2. technical excellence and adherence to sound professional practices, and 3. that projects are completed
within approved parameters of time and budget allotments; interpreting blueprints and technical specifications; preparing change orders, progress reports, and other related documents as required; maintaining fire protection
and suppression methods during construction.

June 1967 - March 1980: full-time employment

D & E Contractors Ltd.
123 Commercial Avenue
Toronto, Ontario

<u>Architectural Draftsperson</u> for this contracting company which specializes in
the construction of educational and commercial structures.

<u>BUSINESS REFERENCES</u>: Available Upon Request.

RESUME #12
CORRECTIONAL OFFICER

Kathleen M. Review
98 Yale Street
Springfield, IL 62756
Home telephone: (217) 782-3333
Business telephone: (217) 782-4444

PERSONAL INFORMATION

Birth date: October 31, 1965
Marital status: married   Dependents: none
Height: 5' 11"   Weight: 160 lbs.
Health: excellent
Citizenship: American
Social Security Number: 123-12-1234

EDUCATIONAL BACKGROUND

B.A. in Psychology (magna cum laude), University of Chicago, Chicago, Illinois,
  1986
  Minor: Philosophy

Diploma (Grade 12 Academic): Frank Towers High School, Chicago, Illinois, 1982

GOVERNMENT SPONSORED WORKSHOPS ATTENDED

Hostage Negotiation Training Program: sponsored by Illinois State Prison,
  (in-house training), Springfield, Illinois, 1990

AVAILABILITY: Minimum of two weeks' notice required.

SALARY EXPECTED: Open — nature and challenge of position itself is of principal concern.

PROFESSIONAL EXPERIENCE

October 1986 - present: full-time employment
  Illinois State Prison
  P.O. Box 2140
  Springfield, Illinois

Correctional Officer, working at this maximum security federal government institution which has approximately 500 male inmates serving sentences ranging
from two years to life imprisonment.

Principal duties and responsibilities involve the following:

Handling Admission Procedures: Responsible for handling matters pertaining
to inmate admission procedures (i.e., completing documentation; listing all
items of personal property, including clothing and monies; issuing institutional clothing; inspecting for contraband, injuries, and/or signs of drug
or alcohol abuse; conducting frisk, dormitory and cell searches; key handling; operating the central control panel; providing basic training to new
recruits on security procedures, etc.);

Security: Responsible for keeping abreast of various government statutes,
acts and orders pertaining to matters of security (e.g., Civil Service Act,
Corrections Act, Civil Rights Act, Privacy Act, Public Service Labor Relations Act, Ombudsman Act, Parole Act & Regulations and Criminal Code of the
United States, as well as for having familiarity with the Criminal Records

Act, Narcotic Control Act, and the Penitentiary & Reformatories Act); ensuring the safe custody and control of inmates until they are legally permitted to leave the institution; transporting inmates from the institution by van to city hospitals for medical care and treatment, or to other types of institutions; ensuring that proper security procedures are in place at all times and strictly adhered to;

Managing The Behavior Of Offenders: Responsible for assessing the needs of offenders at any given time in their sentence (i.e., mental, emotional, physical, social); investigating the psycho-social histories of offenders in order to facilitate more purposeful communication; discussing and resolving problems with offenders, with respect and dignity shown at all times to those concerned, regardless of their type of offense or ethnic background; discussing various program resources with offenders that may be of help to them in facilitating their reintegration within the community upon release;

Non-Violent Crisis Intervention: Responsible for providing non-violent crisis intervention services on attempted suicides, as well as for offenders experiencing severe emotional and/or psychiatric problems; detecting and diffusing potential problems in a professional manner;

Preparing Reports And Recommendations: Responsible for maintaining a daily log of interviews conducted; preparing detailed confidential reports on cases handled, as well as making recommendations to the Review Board, Parole Board, Temporary Absence Board and Transfer Board; participating in the inmate grievance process; maintaining up-to-date records on approved and denied Temporary Absences.

BUSINESS AND CHARACTER REFERENCES: Available Upon Request.

109

RESUME #13
COURT STENOGRAPHER

Quentin A. Quick
43 Litigation Avenue
Halifax, Nova Scotia
B3J 2Y4

Home telephone: (902) 424-1111

PERSONAL INFORMATION

Birth date: March 21, 1968
Health: excellent

EDUCATIONAL BACKGROUND

Diploma (Grade 12 Academic): Peak High School, Halifax, Nova Scotia, 1986

PROFESSIONAL EXPERIENCE

September 4, 1986 - present
        Court of Queen's Bench Nova Scotia
        770 Main Street
        Halifax, Nova Scotia

Court Stenographer. Reporting directly to the Supervising Court Reporter, principal duties and responsibilities involve the following:

Attending Discoveries And Courtroom Proceedings: Responsible for recording, transcribing and typing discoveries (i.e., pre-trial conferences between lawyers and eligible witnesses) and courtroom proceedings held in family court, small claims court and the Court of Queen's Bench trial division, with careful attention to their thoroughness, legality, and completeness; attending criminal and civil courtroom proceedings in order to record evidence and make accurate notes regarding all pertinent facts (i.e., opening remarks, facts of court cases and/or discoveries, names of witnesses, exhibit lists, direct and cross-examinations of witnesses, summary remarks, etc.); transcribing verbatim the oral decisions of Judges; maintaining a list of attendance on jurors;

Maintaining Exhibit Lists: Responsible for dating and marking exhibits for identification, as well as filing of same with the Clerk's Office.

BUSINESS REFERENCE

Mr. Justice B. Gerald Pope
Court of Queen's Bench of Nova Scotia
123 St. Anne Street
Halifax, Nova Scotia
Office telephone: (902) 424-0101

RESUME #14
CREDIT COLLECTION CLERK

Lloyd C. Profit
44 Debit Lane
Lansing, MI 48909

Home telephone: (517) 334-7777

PERSONAL INFORMATION

Birth date: July 25, 1964   Marital status: married   Dependents: one
Height: 6'   Weight: 180 lbs.

EDUCATIONAL BACKGROUND

Diploma (Grade 12 Academic): Lansing High School, Lansing, Michigan, 1982

COMPANY SPONSORED WORKSHOPS AND SEMINARS ATTENDED

Credit & Collections Seminars," provided through ABC Transport Company Ltd.,
    and attended on an ongoing basis throughout my working career

BUSINESS EXPERIENCE

October 1976 - present: full-time employment

    ABC Transport Company Ltd.
    1234 1st Avenue
    Lansing, Michigan

Collection Clerk for this truck transportation company which has thirty-two
terminals situated throughout the United States.Reporting directly to the
Branch Manager, principal duties and responsibilities involve handling approximately 1,000 independent accounts (i.e., grocery distributors; wholesalers and retailers; petroleum companies; automobile dealerships, mining companies, etc.); acting as a liaison between the company and its key customer
accounts on matters pertaining to fiscal responsibility; verifying the ability and determining the willingness of clients to honor their financial obligations on past due accounts, without litigation, when possible (e.g., analyzing financial statements; conducting credit checks and personal
interviews; collecting on current and past due accounts, etc.); making corrections on billing statements; submitting statements of uncollectible accounts to upper management levels; handling applications for credit from new
customers; opening and closing charge accounts; working out payment schedules with clients.
Note: Throughout my employment, I consistently surpassed all monthly collection quotas established by the company.

BUSINESS REFERENCES: Available Upon Request.

RESUME #15
DENTAL ASSISTANT

Monique E. Sparkle
1234 Chemin Chambly
Longueuil, Quebec
G1R 4Y5

Home telephone: (418) 643-3333

PERSONAL INFORMATION

Birth date: August 25, 1949
Marital status: married   Dependents: two teenagers
Height: 5' 3"   Weight: 135 lbs.
Health: excellent

EDUCATIONAL BACKGROUND

Diploma in Dental Assisting: Quebec Institute of Technology, Montreal, Quebec,
   1969

Diploma of Collegiate Studies (College d'Enseignement General et Professionel):
   Gaspe Peninsula College, Gaspe, Quebec, 1968

SPECIAL CERTIFICATE: Intra-Oral Procedures Certificate, sponsored by the Quebec
   Dental Association, and taken through the University of Montreal, Montreal,
   Quebec, 1975

SPECIAL SKILLS AND ABILITIES: Can competently operate the following medical
   equipment: orthopan, x-ray exposing and developing equipment; autoclave;
   sharpener; model trimmer; and ultrasound.

PROFESSIONAL AFFILIATIONS

Canadian Dental Nurses' & Assistants Association, member since 1981
   Quebec Dental Assistants' Association, member since 1981

PROFESSIONAL EXPERIENCE

September 1969 – present: full-time employment
   Dr. A.B. Drill, Dentist
   99 Denture Street
   Lennoxville, Quebec

Dental Assistant, with the responsibility for four-handed chairside assisting, as well as rubber dam application and removal, radiographic exposure
and processing, oral hygiene instruction, application of anticarcinogenic
agents, impression taking for study models, developing x-rays, and some lab
duties.

BUSINESS REFERENCES: Available Upon Request.

RESUME #16
DEPARTMENT STORE MANAGER

Norman F. Storey
184 Douglas Street
Victoria, British Columbia
V8W 3E6
Home telephone: (604) 387-0000

PERSONAL INFORMATION

Birth date: August 18, 1964
Marital status: married   Dependents: two

EDUCATIONAL BACKGROUND

Diploma (Grade 12 Academic): City High School, Victoria, British Columbia, 1983

SPECIAL SKILLS AND ABILITIES

- Have strong organizing, managing, and motivating skills
- Can present a professional company image to clients, fellow workers, subordinates and/or peers

PROFESSIONAL INTERESTS: reading the FINANCIAL POST, THE GLOBE AND MAIL, and business journals dealing with various aspects of marketing

HOBBIES AND INTERESTS: meeting people; reading literature; physical fitness

AVAILABILITY: Minimum of two weeks' notice required.

SALARY EXPECTED: Open — nature and challenge of position itself is of principal concern.

BUSINESS EXPERIENCE

July 1983 - present: full-time employment
  The Victorian Department Store
  123 McKenzie Avenue
  Victoria, British Columbia

Store Manager of this retail operation which has approximately 120 staff members employed in the following departments: Pharmacy, Hardware/Auto, Houseware, Clothing Fashions, Jewellery, Cosmetics, Health & Beauty, Staples, Baby Care, Floral, Entertainment, Photo/Video, Snackbar, and Stationery.

[Promoted from the position of **Store Manager Trainee** (July 1983 - November 1984) to **Group Merchandiser** (November 1984 - June 1985) to the position of **Store Manager** (June 1985 - present)]

Reporting directly to the District Manager on business objectives and results, principal duties and responsibilities as Store Manager involve the following:

Staff Supervision: Responsible for supervising the activities of approximately 120 employees working in the various departments listed above (e.g., planning and scheduling of workloads; assigning tasks; establishing priorities; conducting follow-ups to ensure that assignments are properly completed; providing

adequate motivation to ensure their abilities are fully utilized; promoting
a working environment that is conducive to greater learning and involvement
in order to ensure a minimum turnover of staff);

Public Relations: Responsible for personally resolving telephone inquiries
or complaints from the general public in a polite and professional manner
(i.e., on matters pertaining to sales, lost goods, damages, returns, etc.);
meeting with the representatives of major suppliers on a regular basis in
order to negotiate the best possible prices on stock to be purchased, delivery times, and other pertinent matters pertaining to inventory purchases;
promoting public awareness of the company through good customer service;

Sales Promotion: Responsible for developing weekly specials and competitive
pricing programs; creating and developing promotional concepts and plans, as
well as in-house advertising themes for special seasons and occasions such
as Christmas, New Years', and Mother's Day, etc.; ensuring effective placement of point-of-sale items and planogram in order to ensure a maximization
of profit in the store; ensuring an orderly movement of merchandise in the
store by utilizing the inventory control system efficiently (i.e., pricing,
overstocks, markdowns, carry-over policies, etc.); interpreting the significance of ratings found in NIELSEN MARKETING RESEARCH REPORTS, etc.;

Conducting Staff Meetings: Responsible for conducting weekly staff meetings
which are held in order to evaluate the merits of past sales achievements
and to establish new sales targets.

Special Sales Achievements: Won the Outstanding Manager Award in 1990 (and
was runner-up in 1991) for top store sales and profit in competitions held
among 13 Victorian Department Stores.

Note: This position requires an ability to work with confidence, accuracy,
efficiency, and understanding under all types of pressure situations; and
throughout my employment, I have consistently scored high on all Performance
Evaluations conducted by my supervisor.

BUSINESS REFERENCES: Available Upon Request.

RESUME #17
ELECTRICIAN

Victor B. Volt
321 Electric Avenue
Tallahassee, FL 32301
Home telephone: (904) 487-0000

PERSONAL INFORMATION

Birth date: May 12, 1950
Height: 5' 10"   Weight: 190 lbs.
Health: excellent

EDUCATIONAL BACKGROUND

Trade Qualification in Electrical Construction (Class 3): Fort Lauderdale Institute of Trades, Fort Lauderdale, Florida, April 13, 1972

Diploma: Key West Vocational School, Key West, Florida, June 1968

SPECIAL SKILLS AND ABILITIES

— Can competently operate the following electrical measuring instruments: ammeters, voltmeters, wattmeters, power factor meters, protective relays, oscilloscope, digital tachometers and wheatstone bridge.

UNION MEMBERSHIP

American Paperworkers Union, member since 1978

PROFESSIONAL INTERESTS: reading technical publications on the field of elec
  tronics; PLC (Programmable Logic Controllers for Industrial Computers)

AVAILABILITY: Immediate.

PROFESSIONAL EXPERIENCE

July 1978 - January 1991: full-time employment
  Electrical Industries Ltd.
  10012 - 94th Avenue
  Tallahassee, Florida

Journeyman Electrician for this electrical and instrumentation contracting
company.

Principal duties and responsibilities involved the following:

ELECTRICAL REPAIRS: Responsible for serving as a trouble-shooter for the purpose of diagnosing and repairing complex electrical malfunctions (e.g., performing detailed functional and component part inspections); interpreting
blueprints; working in cooperation with other tradespeople on the completion
of assignments;

OPERATING A PLC SYSTEM: Responsible for operating, programming, and troubleshooting on a Modicom PLC System, as well as providing maintenance repairs
to the system when required [i.e., developing new techniques for on-line PLC
communications; preparing test data for new production programs and verifying the results; preparing guides, tables, charts and various reports; troubleshooting problems encountered with hardware and software and advising
technical experts of suspected problems; etc.).

<u>Note</u>: Have a working knowledge of both the hardware and software pertaining to this PLC System, as well as a knowledge of its conventional relay switching systems and instrumentation.

<u>JUST IN TIME/TOTAL QUALITY CONTROL</u>: Responsible for the ongoing inspection of the quality of personal work completed in order to ensure technical excellence, conformance to requirements, and adherence to sound professional practices; planning and scheduling of personal workloads in order to ensure prompt and timely handling of same.

July 1975 – July 1978: full-time temporary employment
Underground Mining Co.
45 Sandy Avenue
Key West, Florida

<u>Electrician</u> for this company which specializes in mining exploration and development.

June 1972 – July 1975: full-time employment
Bell Tel
15 Alma Street
Key West, Florida

<u>Circuit Installer</u>

<u>BUSINESS REFERENCE</u>
Mr. Jim Shock, Senior Maintenance Man
Electrical Industries Ltd.
10012 - 94th Avenue
Tallahassee, Florida
Business telephone: (904) 487-2222

RESUME #18
ELECTRONICS TECHNOLOGIST

Samuel P. Circuit
967 3rd Street
Toronto, Ontario
M7B 2H6
Home telephone: (416) 596-1234

PERSONAL INFORMATION

Birth date: November 4, 1961
Marital status: single   Dependents: none
Height: 5' 11"   Weight: 165 lbs.
Health: excellent

EDUCATIONAL BACKGROUND

Electronics Engineering Technology — Industrial Diploma: Toronto Community College, Toronto, Ontario, 1983 – 1986

Diploma (Grade 12 Academic): Pearson Senior High School, Toronto, Ontario, 1983

COMPANY SPONSORED TRAINING

Industry Field Engineering Entry Level Training (Drives & Controls Option): sponsored by Security Systems Inc., and held at their Training Center in Schenectady, New York, U.S.A., January 14, 1991 – May 21, 1991

Theoretical & Practical Training in the following areas:
- Variable Speed Drives
- PLC Skills
- Motors and Generators
- Solid State Power Conversion Systems
- Transformers
- Protective Relays
- Switchgear
- Electrical and Insulation Tests

SPECIAL SKILLS AND ABILITIES

— Can competently operate the following electrical measuring instruments: ammeters, voltmeters, wattmeters, megger, chart recorder, impedance bridge, oscilloscope, digital tachometers, high current clamp-on meters

AVAILABILITY: Immediate.

PROFESSIONAL EXPERIENCE

December 1986 – January 1991: full-time employment
        Security Systems Inc.
        312 Alarm Lane
        Toronto, Ontario

Electronics Technologist for this company which repairs electronic security systems. Reporting directly to the Supervisor on work objectives and results, principal duties and responsibilities involved the following:

Client Relations: Responsible for handling the inquiries, concerns, and/or complaints of clients in person or over the telephone in a polite and professional manner; promoting public awareness of the company through good client service;

Electronic/Electrical Repairs: Responsible for serving as a trouble-shooter for the purpose of diagnosing and repairing complex electronic/electrical malfunctions on electronic security systems consisting of close circuit television systems, cameras, access control systems, motion detectors, smoke detectors, and magnetic doorlocks, as well as diagnosing and repairing electronic/electrical malfunctions in intercom systems, PLC systems, emergency lighting units, and power distribution equipment (e.g., troubleshooting for complex electrical/electronic failures; performing detailed functional and component part inspections; performing start-up and tune-up procedures on variable speed drives; repairing control circuits; performing infrared surveys; conducting insulation tests and various other tests on transformers, motors and switchgear; installing and testing 3-Phase breakers; interpreting schematics; etc.);

Just In Time/Total Quality Control: Responsible for the ongoing inspection of the quality of personal work completed in order to ensure: **1.** conformance to requirements; **2.** technical excellence and adherence to sound professional practices, and **3.** that projects are completed within approved parameters of time and budget allotments.

Reason for leaving: Staff cutbacks due to poor market conditions; desire a position which provides ample opportunities for professional growth and continual self-development.

BUSINESS AND CHARACTER REFERENCES: Available Upon Request.

William F. Reynolds
23 Willow Lane
Topeka, KS 66612

Home telephone: (913) 296-2000

PERSONAL INFORMATION

Birth date: July 12, 1951
Marital status: single   Dependents: none
Height: 5' 11"   Weight: 185 lbs.
Health: excellent

EDUCATIONAL BACKGROUND

Bachelor of Engineering Degree (Civil): Topeka Technical College, Topeka, Kansas,
  1973 – 1975
B.Sc., Topeka University, Topeka, Kansas, 1969 – 1973
  Major: Physics
Diploma (Grade 12   Academic): Topeka High School, Topeka, Kansas, 1969

PROFESSIONAL AFFILIATIONS

Association of Professional Engineers of Kansas, member since 1977

American Society for Civil Engineering, member since 1980

TRAVEL: Willing to comply with all travelling requirements; have own car.

RELOCATE: Willing to relocate.

SPECIAL TRAINING: Willing to undergo any amount of special training deemed
  necessary to more adequately meet the continuing demands of this position.

PROFESSIONAL EXPERIENCE

July 1989 – present
  Public Works Department
  P.O. Box 123
  Topeka, Kansas

Project Manager, with the responsibility for directing a staff of architects, engineers, and technical and inspection personnel working on the construction, modifications, and additions of a 240 cell maximum security correctional facility.

<u>Operating Budget</u>: $50 Million
Specific responsibilities involve the following:

Overseeing Project Activities: Responsible for planning, organizing and directing a number of concurrent consultant and construction contracts respecting the following projects: site preparation; foundations and structure; cladding & roofing; interior mechanical and electrical; living units; tunnel; gate house; tower; sewage lagoon; water reservoir; perimeter fence; access road & site landing; renovations to existing buildings; construction & installation of a woodworking factory; modifications to back-up power systems; and installation of an air conditioning sub-system;

Staff Supervision: Responsible for supervising the on-site activities of two Engineers and four Trade Inspectors; supervising the off-site activities of one Architect, three Engineers, on-staff members of the Public Works Department, and an Architectural Consultant;

Just In Time/Total Quality Control: Responsible for providing guidance and advice on administrative problems and matters related to the various projects; ongoing inspection of the quality of work completed by trades and subtrades people in order to ensure 1. technical excellence and adherence to sound professional practices, and 2. that projects are completed within approved parameters of time and budget allotments; preparing progress reports, change orders and payments, and other related reports as required; discussing and resolving with state and federal bodies problems related to design, by-laws, codes, state planning and organizing.

July 1975 – July 1989
Kansas Power Corporation
(Design & Construction Division)
Topeka, Kansas

Senior Construction Engineer, with the responsibility for the management of all civil engineering construction of new substations and modifications to existing substations throughout the State of Kansas.
Note: Projects were valued at approximately $3 Million. Work included site clearing and preparation, roads and rail spurs, concrete foundations, buildings and services, as well as issuing tenders and contracts.

BUSINESS REFERENCES: Available Upon Request.

Russell G. Green
52 Grain Road
Madison, WI 53707

Home telephone: (608) 266-4444

PERSONAL INFORMATION

Birth date: June 13, 1947
Health: excellent

EDUCATIONAL BACKGROUND

Agricultural Diploma: Madison Agricultural College, Madison, Wisconsin,
   1965 - 1967

Areas of concentration:
- Green House Management
- Crop Production
- Vegetable Production
- Soil Science
- Plant Science
- Agricultural Financing
- Animal Science
- Structural Engineering

Diploma: West District High School, Madison, Wisconsin, 1965

SPECIAL SKILLS AND ABILITIES

- Possess strong interpersonal communication skills, and have a demonstrated interest in working harmoniously with others
- Can present a professional company image to clients, fellow workers, subordinates and/or peers

PROFESSIONAL AFFILIATIONS

Holstein United States, Madison, Wisconsin, active member since 1975
   Madison Soil & Crop Improvement Association, Madison, Wisconsin
   Served as President from 1987 - present

AGRICULTURAL WORKSHOPS AND SEMINARS ATTENDED

Tillage Day, sponsored by the Madison Soil & Crop Improvement
   Association, and held in Madison, Wisconsin, May 6, 1989
   Silage Technology & Management Workshop, sponsored by the United States Department of Agriculture, and held in Truro, Nova Scotia, Canada, March 29 -
   30, 1989

AGRICULTURAL SYMPOSIUMS ATTENDED

National Forage Symposium, sponsored by the United States Department of Agriculture, and held in Madison, Wisconsin, November 24 - 26, 1981

Large Herd Symposium, sponsored by the Ontario Ministry of Agriculture and Food
   & Agriculture Canada, and held in Ottawa, Ontario, Canada, November 22 - 24,
   1981

AGRICULTURAL EXPOSITION ATTENDED

World Dairy Exposition (i.e., an international livestock exposition) sponsored
   by the United States Department of Agriculture and University of Wisconsin,
   and held in Madison, Wisconsin, September 29 - October 4, 1987

PROFESSIONAL INTERESTS: keeping abreast of political and economic issues pertaining to the agricultural industry (i.e., market trends, business cycles,
   and economic indicators,. etc.)

PROFESSIONAL EXPERIENCE

June 1967 - January 1991: full-time employment
   Holstein Dairy Farm
   Madison, Wisconsin

   Total Farm Acreage: 280 (Cleared & Wooded)

   Approximate Number of Dairy Cattle: up to 250

   Average Number Of Hours Of Work Per Week: 49

   Manager of this farm which specializes in milk production, and provides
   custom combining and fieldwork services to community-based farms on a con-
   tractual basis. Principal duties and responsibilities involved the following:

   STAFF SUPERVISION: Responsible for supervising the activities of five full-
   time staff members, as well as seasonal employees;

   CARE & TRANSPORTATION OF LIVESTOCK: Responsible for providing for the care
   of livestock, as well as their transportation to various locations within
   the state of Wisconsin;

   GENERAL MAINTENANCE WORK: Responsible for safely operating and maintaining a
   computerized feeding system, a feed mill, a seed mill (which has a finished
   product capacity of two tons per hour), a five-ton truck and four tractors;
   maintaining the land, buildings and farm equipment (i.e., damage repairs of
   an electrical or mechanical nature; carpentry work, etc.).

BUSINESS AND CHARACTER REFERENCES: Available Upon Request.

RESUME #21
FINANCIAL PLANNER

Sarah M. Rich
321 Profit Avenue
Ottawa, Ontario
K1A 0C9

Home telephone: (819) 997-1058

EDUCATIONAL BACKGROUND

Diploma (Grade 12 Academic): Applewood High School, Ottawa, Ontario, 1984

SPECIAL LICENCES

Chartered Financial Planner Program (CFP), taken through the Canadian Institute
  of Financial Planning, 1985

Investment Funds Institute of Canada (IFIC): sponsored by Financial Planners,
  Ottawa, Ontario, 1984

AVAILABILITY: Minimum of two weeks' notice required.

SALARY EXPECTED: Negotiable.

SALES EXPERIENCE

June 1984 - present: full-time employment

    Financial Planners
    876 Security Boulevard
    Ottawa, Ontario

Financial Planner for this national company which specializes in providing
personal financial planning services to individuals and groups. Reporting directly to the Division Manager, principal duties and responsibilities involve the following:

FINANCIAL COUNSELLING & SALES: Responsible for providing financial counsel-
ling services to clients on Mutual Funds, Life and Term Certain Annuities,
Estate Planning, Money Market Chequing, Guaranteed Investment Certificates,
Investment Funds, Pension Plans, Individual And Group Life And Disability Insurance, Charitable Annuities, Income Deferred Certificates, Tax Exempt
Trusts, Mortgage Loans, Charitable Foundation Trusts, Registered Education
Savings Plans, Registered Retirement Savings Plans, and Registered Retirement Income Funds; selling all of the above mentioned financial products; advising on tax savings strategies; keeping informed and advising clients on
matters pertaining to market trends, business cycles, economic indicators;
interpreting economic and financial journals and monographs; promoting public awareness of the company's services through sound advice and dependable
client service.

BUSINESS REFERENCES: Available Upon Request.

RESUME #22
FLIGHT ATTENDANT

Frank L. Clement
278 Mackenzie Street
Albany, NY 12231

Home telephone: (518) 474-8888

PERSONAL INFORMATION

Birth date: December 25, 1968
Marital status: single   Dependents: none
Height: 5' 11"   Weight: 170 lbs.

EDUCATIONAL BACKGROUND

Diploma: City Center High School, Albany, New York, 1986

COMPANY SPONSORED PROGRAM

Flight Attendant Initial Training Program, taken through Eagle Airlines (Training Center), New York City, New York, July 1986
Duration: four weeks of intensive training

SPECIAL SKILLS AND ABILITIES

- Can present a professional company image to passengers, fellow workers, subordinates, peers and/or passengers

RESERVE DUTY: Willing to work on call twenty-four hours per day.

AVAILABILITY: Minimum of two weeks' notice required.

SALARY EXPECTED: Open — nature and challenge of position itself is of principal concern.

PROFESSIONAL EXPERIENCE

July 1986 – present: full-time employment

Eagle Airlines Ltd.
123 Main Street
Albany, New York

Flight Attendant for this international airlines company. Principal duties
and responsibilities involve the following: attending to the safety and
needs of passengers (i.e., preparing drinks, serving meals, handling customer inquiries, concerns, and/or complaints in a polite and professional manner, etc.); promoting public awareness of the airlines through good passenger service.
Note: This position requires an ability to work with confidence, poise, and
efficiency under all types of pressure situations.

BUSINESS AND CHARACTER REFERENCES: Available Upon Request.

RESUME #23
GRAPHIC ARTIST

Brian R. Knack
123 Picture Crescent
Dover, DE 19901

Home telephone: (302) 736-3073

EDUCATIONAL BACKGROUND
B.A., University of Dover, Dover, Delaware, 1979
        Major: Fine Arts, Visual
Diploma (Grade 12 Academic): Dover High School, Dover, Delaware, 1975

PROFESSIONAL EXPERIENCE
September 1979 – present
        A & B Graphics Ltd.
        1401 9th Street
        Dover, Delaware

Graphic Artist, working in the silk screen plant, for this company which specializes in the design of annual reports, prospectuses, brochures, and in-house organs through to camera-ready art.

Reporting directly to the Manager on work objectives and results, principal duties and responsibilities involve the following:

Graphic Artwork: Responsible for interviewing customers in order to ascertain the types of graphic artwork concepts they would like to have introduced into their business plans; planning the design work of graphic illustrations and preparing customer presentations (i.e., drafting & rendering of drawings and design work; fabric surface design; silkscreen printing; tie dying; preparing saturated and pale dye color charts; etchings; relief; embossments; using computer assisted drafting techniques; etc.).

Special Award: In 1991, received the company's "Award of Excellence."

BUSINESS REFERENCES: Available Upon Request.

ADDITIONAL REMARKS: A complete dossier of my graphic art projects is available upon request.

RESUME #24
GROCERY STORE MANAGER

Gabrielle C. Grocer
98 Produce Drive
Sacramento, CA 91234

Home telephone: (916) 324-1000

EDUCATIONAL BACKGROUND

Diploma (Grade 12 Academic): Dr. Brown High School, Sacramento, California, 1970

SPECIAL SKILLS AND ABILITIES

- Can plan workloads and supervise subordinates to the best advantage
- Have a strong knowledge of office practice and procedure
- Can present a professional company image to clients, fellow workers, subordinates and/or peers

TRAVEL: Willing to comply with all travelling requirements.

SPECIAL TRAINING: Willing to undergo any amount of special training deemed necessary to more adequately meet the continuing demands of this position.

AVAILABILITY: Minimum of two weeks' notice required.

PRESENT EMPLOYER: My present employer is currently unaware of my decision to seek other employment; however, he may be contacted to answer any questions about my work record, after first notifying myself of your intention to do so.

BUSINESS EXPERIENCE

July 1975 – present: full-time employment
A & B Groceries
321 Rose Boulevard
Sacramento, California

Merchandising Supervisor, with the responsibility for managing all activities pertaining to the efficient operation of this retail grocery store.

Reporting directly to the Area Supervisor on business objectives and results, principal duties and responsibilities involve the following:

STAFF SUPERVISION: Responsible for supervising the activities of approximately 120 employees, among whom included Department Heads, Cashiers, Maintenance and Janitorial Staff, Clerks, Clerk Typists, and an Accountant (e.g., interpreting policy and procedure issued from the Board of Directors and ensuring staff compliance with directives; planning and scheduling of workloads; conducting follow-ups to ensure that assignments are properly completed; promoting a working environment that is conducive to greater learning and involvement in order to ensure a minimum turnover of staff);

PUBLIC RELATIONS: Responsible for personally resolving telephone inquiries or complaints from the general public in a polite and professional manner, when required (i.e., on matters pertaining to sales, lost goods, damages, returns, etc.); promoting public awareness of the company through good customer service;

126

<u>CREATING & DEVELOPING ADVERTISING & PROMOTIONAL CONCEPTS</u>: Responsible for managing all phases of the company's Consumers Advertising Flyer which has a weekly circulation of 120,000 - 130,000, in order to ensure a maximization of profit in the company; developing weekly specials and competitive pricing programs; developing and coordinating a competitive every-day-low-price program for areas served, etc.);

<u>SALES PROMOTION</u>: Responsible for setting-up Product Knowledge Training Sessions for company staff; ensuring that display areas on product lines are properly set-up (i.e., that proper attention has been given to their design, layout, color schemes and decor; ensuring effective placement of point of sale items and planogram, etc. in order to ensure a maximization of profit in the store); ensuring an orderly movement of merchandise in the store by utilizing the inventory control system efficiently (i.e., pricing, overstocks, markdowns, carry-over policies, etc.).

June 1970 - July 1975: full-time employment
A.B.C. Groceries Ltd.
123 Commercial Avenue
Sacramento, California

<u>Produce Manager</u> for this grocery store which has 50 employees.

<u>BUSINESS AND CHARACTER REFERENCES</u>: Available Upon Request.

HOCKEY ASSOCIATION PRESIDENT/PROFESSIONAL HOCKEY PLAYER

Ulysses P. Puck
333 Board Drive
Moncton, New Brunswick
E1A 5K7

Home telephone: (506) 382-0000

PERSONAL INFORMATION

Birth date: March 30, 1960
Height: 5' 8"   Weight: 165 lbs.
Health: excellent
Citizenship: Canadian

EDUCATIONAL BACKGROUND

Diploma (Grade 12 Academic): Vanier High School, Moncton, New Brunswick, 1978

PROFESSIONAL EXPERIENCE

April 1988 - present: full-time employment

Minor Hockey Association
Moncton, New Brunswick

President: Acting under the direction of the Chairperson of the Board and the
   Operations Council, principal duties and responsibilities involve the following: representing the Minor Hockey Association at the Annual General Meetings of the New Brunswick Amateur Hockey Association; providing proper and
   consistent interpretations of the rules, regulations and bylaws of the New
   Brunswick Amateur Hockey Association; ensuring that the affairs of the Association are conducted in a professional manner and that funds of this Association are properly collected and accounted for; ensuring that the Association acts in compliance with the operational policies and procedures defined
   by the New Brunswick Amateur Hockey Association; updating the Association's
   Constitution as required.

September 1978 - April 1988: fulltime employment

   The Moncton Eagles
   Moncton, New Brunswick

Professional Hockey Player for this affiliate of the Winnipeg Hawks (NHL).

NOTE: Served as Team Captain in 1988; and from 1985 - 1988, served as an Assistant Captain.

RESUME #26
HOME ECONOMIST

Viola D. Cook
987 Textile Avenue
Topeka, KS 66612

Home telephone: (913) 296-2222

PERSONAL INFORMATION
Birth date: June 13, 1954

EDUCATIONAL BACKGROUND
Bachelor of Home Economics, Topeka University (School of Nutrition & Family
  Studies), Topeka, Kansas, 1977
  Area of concentration: Education

  Diploma (Grade 12 Academic): Wichita High School, Wichita, Kansas, 1972

PROFESSIONAL ASSOCIATION
Kansas State Home Economics Association, active member since 1978

VOLUNTEER WORK
Topeka Home Economics Convention, served on the Planning Committee in the Fall
  of 1991

SPECIAL TRAINING: Willing to undergo any amount of special training deemed necessary to more adequately meet the continuing demands of this position.

TRAVEL: Willing to comply with all travelling requirements; have own car.

HOBBIES AND INTERESTS: nutrition; reading literature; craftwork

AVAILABILITY: Minimum of two weeks' notice required.

SALARY EXPECTED: Open — nature and challenge of position itself is of principal concern.

PROFESSIONAL EXPERIENCE
May 1977 - present: full-time employment
  United States Department of Agriculture
  P.O. Box 321
  Topeka, Kansas

Home Economist, with the responsibility for promoting consumer education in
the area of home management. Reporting directly to the Home Economist Supervisor and District Agriculturalist, principal duties and responsibilities involve the following:

Setting Up Educational Workshops And Programs: Responsible for setting up
workshops and programs on nutrition, interior decorating, family finance,
crafts, metric system, energy conservation, sewing and textile care; developing procedures to identify those areas where goals or services have been successfully attained;

Public Relations: Responsible for answering in a polite and professional manner inquiries from the general public; researching, preparing and recording a five minute agricultural broadcast that was aired once a week over the local radio station; promoting public awareness of available programs through effective advertising campaigns;

Preparing Media Kits And Press Releases: Responsible for creating and developing information packages to advertise the availability of the programs to the general public; preparing media kits and press releases; maintaining a bank of information on the times, dates, and locations of planned events; preparing slide shows, audio/video presentations, and lectures; researching and writing articles for local newspapers and an agricultural newsletter;

Attending Trade Shows And Market Places: Responsible for representing the Department of Agriculture at Trade Shows and Market Places held throughout the State of Kansas, for the purpose of promoting consumer education in the area of home management.

BUSINESS REFERENCE

Mrs. Alice Trainor, Home Economist Supervisor
United States Department of Agriculture
P.O. Box 321
Topeka, Kansas
Business telephone: (913) 296-1111

RESUME #27
INSURANCE CLERK

Wendell P. Claims
33 Indemnity Lane
Oklahoma City, OK 73105

Home telephone: (405) 521-3911

PERSONAL INFORMATION

Birth date: August 27, 1959
Marital status: married   Dependents: none
Health: excellent

EDUCATIONAL BACKGROUND

Diploma (Grade 12 Academic): Tulsa Public High School, Tulsa, Oklahoma, 1977

INSURANCE COURSES COMPLETED (Sponsored by National Insurance Ltd.)

   Principles and Practices; Automobile Insurance; Insurance On Property, Part
   I; Insurance Against Liability; Loss Adjustments & Claims Settlements; Bodily Injury Claims; Casualty Covers

SPECIAL SKILLS AND ABILITIES

* Possess strong interpersonal communication skills, and have a demonstrated
  interest in working harmoniously with others
* Can organize own personal time and tasks efficiently
* Possess strong analytical, mathematical, and statistical skills
* Can present a professional company image to clients, fellow workers, subor-
  dinates and/or peers

SPECIAL TRAINING: Willing to undergo any amount of special training deemed necessary to more adequately meet the continuing demands of this position.

HOBBIES AND INTERESTS: meeting people; reading literature; physical fitness;
   playing the piano

AVAILABILITY: Minimum of two weeks' notice required.

SALARY EXPECTED: Open — nature and challenge of position itself is of principal concern.

BUSINESS EXPERIENCE

June 25, 1977 - present: full-time employment
   National Insurance Ltd.
   35 Insurance Lane
   Oklahoma City, Oklahoma

System Service/Premium Listing Clerk for this company which specializes in
the sale of automobile insurance.

Reporting directly to the Unit Supervisor on business objectives and results, principal duties and responsibilities involve the following:

131

PUBLIC RELATIONS: Responsible for answering in a polite and professional manner the inquiries, complaints, needs and/or concerns of policyholders, sales representatives, lienholders/mortgagees, service and claims representatives, and representatives of the motor vehicle branch, as well as ensuring that such problems are promptly addressed through the appropriate personnel; acting as a contact for the Accounting Unit on matters pertaining to irregularities in accounts receivable or invalid accounts; promoting public awareness of the company through good customer service;

OFFICE ADMINISTRATION: Responsible for maintaining a working knowledge of the various Acts governing insurance practices; preparing and balancing all accounting documents; accepting new business applications; examining applications for accuracy of completion and premium; reviewing the transmittals of agents; ordering Inspection Reports of applicants and employees; preparing Control Cards and Application Lists; evaluating and posting agents paysheets; preparing Notices of Claim and follow-up correspondence; controlling and distributing leads; preparing legally binding agreements between the buyers of auto insurance and company; acquiring a working knowledge of the general operating procedures of other departments within the company;

COMPUTER APPLICATIONS: Responsible for entering and retrieving data from the company's on-line computer, on matters pertaining to Monthly Pay Plan and policyholders, etc.; troubleshooting problems encountered with hardware/software and advising Systems Analysts of suspected problems.

BUSINESS AND CHARACTER REFERENCES: Available Upon Request.

RESUME #28
INVENTORY CONTROL CLERK

Richard J. Goods
123 Requisition Lane
Frankfort, KY 40601

Home telephone: (502) 564-0000

EDUCATIONAL BACKGROUND

Diploma: West Central High School, Frankfort, Kentucky, 1982

BONDABLE: I am bondable, and can pass a police security check.

AVAILABILITY: Immediate.

WORK EXPERIENCE

May 1986 - January 1991: full-time employment

Palace Hotel
750 Portage Street
Frankfort, Kentucky

Inventory Control Clerk: Principal duties and responsibilities involved
requisitioning, issuing and controlling inventory on all hotel supplies
(i.e., raw materials such as meat and food, bakery supplies, paper products,
janitorial supplies, alcohol and beverages for all banquet rooms and restaurants in the hotel, etc.); signing for goods received, as well as submitting
invoices of such requisitions to the Accounting Department; processing orders and/or claims for damaged or lost goods; ensuring the security of all
supplies (i.e., that proper procedures were followed when locking-up and
storing valuables).

September 1982 - May 1986: full-time employment

Hotel Frankfort
85 Main Street
Frankfort, Kentucky

Busboy, working in the hotel's restaurant. Responsible for cleaning and properly setting up tables.

BUSINESS REFERENCES: Available Upon Request.

RESUME #29
LABORER

Alan K. Loader
9049 St. Thomas Road
Whitehorse, Yukon
Y1A 2C6

Home telephone: (403) 667-2222

PERSONAL INFORMATION
Birth date: June 1, 1959
Height: 5' 11"   Weight: 220 lbs.
Health: excellent

EDUCATIONAL BACKGROUND
Grade 11: Vanier High School, Whitehorse, Yukon, 1986

SHIFTWORK: Willing to work shiftwork.

OVERTIME: Willing to work any amount of overtime.

HOBBIES AND INTERESTS: carpentry, plumbing, physical fitness.

AVAILABILITY: Minimum of two weeks' notice required.

WORK EXPERIENCE
September 1987 - present: full-time employment

    A & C Construction Ltd.
    174 Building Avenue
    Whitehorse, Yukon

    Laborer for this general contracting company. Principal duties and responsi-
    bilities involve assisting trades people on various construction activities
    (i.e., plumbing, carpentry work, roofing, siding, footings, excavating);
    safely operating a tractor with a front end loader, a forklift, and a one
    ton truck; practicing good work habits in order to ensure the occupational
    health and safety of all on-site workers.

June 1986 - September 1987: full-time employment

    Paving & Construction Ltd.
    181 Pavement Lane
    Whitehorse, Yukon

    Flag Person for this company which specializes in the construction and/or
    grading of parking lots and roads, and equipment rentals.

WORK AND CHARACTER REFERENCES: Available Upon Request.

RESUME #30
MILITARY OFFICER

Ronald M. Charge
129 Esquimalt Road
Esquimalt, British Columbia
V8W 3E6

Home telephone: (604) 387-4444

PERSONAL INFORMATION

Birth date: December 31, 1963
Marital status: married   Dependents: two
Height: 6'   Weight: 170 lbs.
Health: excellent

EDUCATIONAL BACKGROUND

Diploma (Grade 12): Superior High School, Victoria, British Columbia, 1981

SPECIAL DRIVER'S LICENCE
Track Vehicles Licence & Wheeled Vehicle Licence for up to five ton trucks and
44 seat passenger buses and tractor trailers

PRESENT EMPLOYER: Present employer is prepared to discuss any questions regarding my work record at this time. (Please refer to the Business References
   provided at the end of this resume for the name, address, and business telephone of individual to contact).

SALARY EXPECTED: Open — nature and challenge of position itself is of principal concern.

WORK EXPERIENCE

October 1981 - present: full-time employment

   Canadian Armed Forces
   CFB Esquimalt
   Esquimalt, British Columbia

   Corporal (Present Job Title)

[Promoted from the position of Private (October 18, 1981 - October 18, 1985)
to the position of Corporal (October 18, 1985 - present)]

Principal duties and responsibilities as a Corporal involve the following:

STAFF SUPERVISION: Responsible for supervising the activities of four subordinates, when required (e.g., interpreting policy and procedure issued from
   top management; planning and scheduling of workloads in order to ensure
   prompt and timely handling of same; assigning tasks; establishing priorities; promoting a working environment that is conducive to greater learning
   and involvement; providing adequate motivation in order to ensure their abilities are fully utilized; developing and maintaining good rapport and effective working relations with all staff members);

<u>ENSURING BUILDINGS & GROUNDS SECURITY</u>: Responsible for investigating and reporting all potential security concerns to the appropriate authorities (i.e., potential security risks to military vehicles, buildings and grounds); ensuring that proper security procedures are in place at all times and strictly adhered to;

<u>EQUIPMENT OPERATIONS</u>: Responsible for the safe and efficient operation of military vehicles (i.e., 44 passenger buses and tractor trailers); operating all communications equipment (i.e., everything from field battery operated switchboards through to solid state switchboards).

<u>Career Objective</u>: Desire a position which provides more opportunities for professional growth and continual self-development.

<u>BUSINESS REFERENCE</u>

Master Corporal Achilles Patton
1234 Tranquillity Lane
Esquimalt, British Columbia
V8W 3E6
Business telephone: (604) 387-5101

<u>CHARACTER REFERENCE</u>

Mr. George Fox, Chartered Accountant
Patton, Price, Fox
987 Baton Avenue
Victoria, British Columbia
Business telephone: (604) 387-1001

<u>ADDITIONAL REMARKS</u>: I am a results-oriented individual, and can work profitably, independently, or in cooperation with others; and I work with enthusiasm and high energy on all assignments.

RESUME #31
NURSE (PUBLIC HEALTH)

Mona W. Comeau
43 Trinity Street
Hartford, CT 06123

Home telephone: (203) 566-2448

PERSONAL INFORMATION

Birth date: September 12, 1949
Marital status: married
Health: excellent

EDUCATIONAL BACKGROUND

B.N.Sc., University of Hartford, Connecticut, 1971
  Area of study: Public Health

Registered Nursing Diploma: The Hartford Hospital School of Nursing, Hartford, Connecticut, 1969

Diploma (Grade 12 Academic): The Hartford High School, Hartford, Connecticut, 1967

PROFESSIONAL AFFILIATIONS

Registered Nurses' Association of Connecticut, Practicing Membership

College of Nurses in Connecticut, Regular Membership

Montessori Parents' Association, active member from 1988 - 1990
  Note: Served as a Chairperson of the Special Events Committee from 1989 - 1990.

WORKSHOPS AND SEMINARS ATTENDED

Ostomy Care Workshop, provided through the Enterostomal Therapy Association of Connecticut, and held at The Hartford Hospital, Hartford, Connecticut, 1991

Maternal Infant Bonding, provided through the University of Hartford, Connecticut, 1991

SPECIAL SKILLS AND ABILITIES

- Possess strong interpersonal communication skills, and have a demonstrated interest in working harmoniously with others
- Can present a professional company image to clients, fellow workers, subordinates and/or the general public

PROFESSIONAL INTERESTS: Reading scientific journals on the nursing profession in order to keep abreast of the ongoing changes, trends, and advances in emergency care and treatment

PROFESSIONAL EXPERIENCE

March 1974 - January 1992

Capital Regional District
1234 Hedley Street
Hartford, Connecticut

Public Health Nurse. Principal duties involved the following:

Public Health: Responsible for assisting in the control of infectious diseases within the community (i.e., AIDS, salmonella, intestinal parasites, food poisoning, tuberculosis, diphtheria, etc.); assisting in the implementation of the state immunization program for both child and adult populations; preparing for and participating in case conferences as required; collecting and organizing data for the health surveillance registry and other health statistical reports; conducting investigative reports on child abuse with other helping professionals;

Evaluating Family Health Needs: Responsible for conducting home visitations to provide consultation services to parents on available community programs and services (i.e., welfare, state hearing and vision departments, long term care facilities, mental health centers, police, alcohol and drug commission, consumer and corporate affairs, etc.); evaluating the holistic health needs of family units and their individual members (i.e., mental, emotional, physical, and social); maintaining a close liaison between parents, hospital staff, family physicians, and other helping professionals; conducting routine developmental, hearing, and vision screening tests;

Teaching: Responsible for instructing newly married couples in prenatal and postnatal classes, as well as providing discussion groups on the role of the Public Health Nurse in the community; providing guest lectures within school settings on such subjects as poison control, socially transmitted diseases, nutrition, birth control, infant care, and babysitting;

Counseling: Responsible for counseling adolescents on their sexuality, personal hygiene, skin care, mental health, family problems, nutrition, menstruation, etc.

September 1971 - March 1974

Hartford Hospital for Children
University Avenue
Hartford, Connecticut

Nurse, working in the poison control centre.

RESUME #32
NURSE (REGISTERED)

Catherine L. Nightingale
26 Holistic Road
Edmonton, Alberta
T5J 3A3

Home telephone: (403) 427-0000

PERSONAL INFORMATION
Birth date: July 25, 1952
Health: excellent

EDUCATIONAL BACKGROUND

Registered Nursing Diploma: the Edmonton Hospital School of Nursing, Edmonton, Alberta, 1970-1973

Diploma (Grade 12 Academic): Edmonton High School, Edmonton, Alberta, 1970

PROFESSIONAL AFFILIATIONS

Canadian Nurses' Society, member in good standing since 1974

The Nurses' Association of Alberta, member in good standing since 1973

Alberta Gerontological Nurses' Association, member in good standing since 1984

PROFESSIONAL INTERESTS: Reading scientific journals on the nursing profession in order to keep abreast of the ongoing changes, trends, and advances in emergency care and treatment

AVAILABILITY: Minimum of one month's notice required.

PROFESSIONAL EXPERIENCE

June 1978 - present: full-time employment
  The Edmonton Hospital
  153 Amend Avenue
  Edmonton, Alberta

Registered Nurse, working in the Emergency, Surgery, Medicine, Orthopedic, and Gynecology Wards of this 539 bed accredited hospital.

Reporting directly to the Doctor on work objectives and results, principal duties and responsibilities involve the following:

Emergency care: Responsible for providing emergency care and treatment to patients (e.g., primary and secondary assessment of casualty victims; cardio-pulmonary resuscitation; treatment of shock, hemorrhaging, fractures; preparing traction splints,etc.)

Attending to the Holistic Health Needs of Patients: Responsible for evaluating and attending to the holistic health needs of patients (i.e., physical, mental, emotional, etc.), with respect and dignity shown at all times to those concerned, regardless of their socio-economic or ethnic background; providing input on care plans designed to return patients to optimal function or to maintain them at their present level of health; advising patients on the significance of various medical problems they may be experiencing in order to help them in their understanding and management of such problems;

139

developing good rapport and effective working relationships with other health care professionals and staff members, as well as providing ongoing consultations to same on the status of personal caseload handled;

Office Administration: Responsible for maintaining a running log of personal cases handled, as well as preparing report analysis; interpreting technical publications; developing and maintaining effective working relationships with all staff members and representatives of management.

September 1973 - June 1978: full time employment

Calgary Hospital
   15 Corrective Street
   Calgary, Alberta

Registered Nurse, working in the Coronary Intensive Care Ward of this 450 bed accredited hospital.

BUSINESS REFERENCES

Dr. David Knowes, Medical Doctor
The Edmonton Hospital
153 Amend Avenue
Edmonton, Alberta
Office telephone: (403) 427-1111

Dr. Pamela Backer, Emergency Room Physician
The Edmonton Hospital
153 Amend Avenue
Edmonton, Alberta
Office telephone: (403) 427-2222

ADDITIONAL REMARKS: I am a results-oriented individual, and can work profitably, independently, or in cooperation with others; and I work with enthusiasm and high energy on all assignments.

RESUME #33
PERSONNEL ADMINISTRATOR

Laura T. Ladd
345 Personnel Lane
Olympia, WA 98504

Home telephone: (206) 753-5555

EDUCATIONAL BACKGROUND

Bachelor of Commerce: University of Olympia, Olympia, Washington, 1973
   Major: Business Administration
   Minor: Economics

Diploma (Grade 12 Academic): West Central High School, Olympia, Washington, 1970

WORKSHOPS AND SEMINARS ATTENDED (Sponsored by City Center Hospital)

Labor Law; Local Administration & Assertiveness; Legislative Procedures; General Labor Relations

SPECIAL SKILLS AND ABILITIES

- Have strong negotiating skills, and am a competent advocate in the field of labor law
- Can plan workloads and supervise subordinates to the best advantage

AVAILABILITY: Minimum of one month's notice required.

PROFESSIONAL EXPERIENCE

August 1973 - present: full-time employment
   City Center Hospital
   123 Care Street
   Olympia, Washington

Director of Personnel for this 550 bed accredited hospital.
Reporting directly to the Executive Director of Human Resources on business objectives and results, principal duties and responsibilities involve the following:

Union/Management Negotiations: Responsible for acting as a liaison between union and management on all matters pertaining to management and employees; collecting and analyzing all pertinent information concerning collective bargaining, and administrating collective agreements; preparing reports with recommendations on compensation and benefit practices and collective agreement negotiations, for the purpose of advising the Board of Management; providing extensive, timely, and accurate information to counsel for arbitration presentations, as well as providing testimonies, as required; developing and implementing all presentations regarding grievance; developing, implementing, and administrating various union guidelines; negotiating corrective or disciplinary action via the grievance procedure; acquiring the support of all local union members on restricting clauses which limited the negative impact on the union; maintaining occupational health and safety standards on behalf of the union; providing advice to members of the local union and others with reference to labor law and various state acts; administering benefit plans for Local Union (490);

Personnel Administration: Responsible for screening and verifying job descriptions issued from various Department Heads; scheduling and conducting interviews with prospective employees, independently and/or in conjunction with Department Heads; chairing group hiring decisions; coordinating vacation times of staff to ensure that the workflow will be properly attended to and uninterrupted in the absence of fellow employees; formulating and implementing absenteeism policies and performance appraisals; assisting staff members with the interpretation of their medical plan benefits and workers' compensation plan benefits; reviewing records of sick leave, leaves-of-absence, leaves-without-pay, lieu time, monthly casual overtime, reclassification, seniority list, and weekly time sheet books;

Preparing Recruitment Budgets: Responsible for preparing recruitment budgets, as well as ensuring that financial allotments for the hiring of new personnel are complied with.

BUSINESS REFERENCE

Dr. Samuel Worth, President, Board of Directors
City Center Hospital
123 Care Street
Olympia, Washington
Business telephone: (206) 753-1111

CHARACTER REFERENCE

Mr. Reginald Bourque, Attorney
Bourque, Landry & Brion
76 Prestige Avenue
Olympia, Washington
Business telephone: (206) 753-2222

PHOTOGRAPHER

Evelyn I. Portrait
91 Picture Lane
Denver, CO 80203

Home telephone: (303) 894-2200

<u>PERSONAL INFORMATION</u>
Birth date: November 22, 1966
Health: excellent

<u>EDUCATIONAL BACKGROUND</u>
Communication Arts Program: ABC College, Denver, Colorado, 1985 - 1987
  <u>Major</u>: Photography
Diploma (Grade 12 Academic): Denver High School, Denver, Colorado, 1984

<u>PROFESSIONAL PHOTOGRAPHERS' CONVENTION ATTENDED</u>
Professional Photographers' Annual Convention, Denver, Colorado, 1987

<u>Special Recognition</u>: Received an Award of Merit for a black & white technical photograph

<u>PROFESSIONAL INTERESTS</u>: calligraphy, pencil sketching, and photography

<u>AVAILABILITY</u>: Minimum of two weeks' notice required.

<u>PRESENT EMPLOYER</u>: My present employer is currently unaware of my decision to seek other employment; however, he may be contacted to answer any questions about my work record, after first notifying myself of your intention to do so.

<u>PROFESSIONAL EXPERIENCE</u>
May 1987 - present: full-time employment

Picture Perfect Photography & Lab
103 Brunswick Street
Denver, Colorado

<u>Assistant Photographer</u>: Duties and responsibilities involve the following: taking pictures; cropping negative and color photos; setting up album proofs for customer presentations (i.e., weddings, beauty pageants, school graduations, family portraits, etc.); preparing slide duplications and inter-negatives; custom printing and developing (i.e., black and white and color photos); selling pictures, frames, folders and accessories; handling customer inquiries and concerns in a polite and professional manner; promoting public awareness of the company through good customer service.

RESUME #35
PILOT

Frank L. Airborne
333 Runway Avenue
Toronto, Ontario
M7A 2H6

Home telephone: (416) 963-4444

PERSONAL INFORMATION

Birth date: August 24, 1962
Marital status: single   Dependents: none
Height: 5' 9"   Weight: 150 lbs.
Health: excellent

Note: I do not have a current or previous illness or disability that will affect my ability to perform the duties and responsibilities of this or any position.

EDUCATIONAL BACKGROUND

Bachelor of Engineering (Electrical): University of Toronto, Toronto, Ontario, 1984

Diploma (Grade 12 Academic): Dr. A. B. Pearce Senior High School, Toronto, Ontario, 1980

PILOT LICENCES

Commercial Pilot's Licence, issued through the Department of Transportation, Ottawa, Ontario, Canada, April 1985

Private Pilot's Licence, issued through the Department of Transportation, Ottawa, Ontario, Canada, April 1982

PROFESSIONAL AFFILIATION

Canadian Owners & Pilots Association, member in good standing since January 1982

HOURS OF FLYING TIME (Private & Commercial)

	HOURS
1. Total Time:	201.4
2. Duel Day:	74.1
3. Duel Night:	5.2
4. Pilot In Command (Day):	104.5
5. Pilot In Command (Night):	17.6
6. Crosscountry:	46.1
7. Instrument & Hood Time:	25.0

SPECIAL SKILLS AND ABILITIES

- Can present a professional company image to passengers, fellow workers and/or peers

TRAVEL: Willing to comply with all travelling requirements.

RESERVE DUTY: Willing to work on call in the absence of fellow employees.

AVAILABILITY: Minimum of two weeks' notice required.

PROFESSIONAL EXPERIENCE

July 1988 - present: full-time employment
  Airlines International Flight Centre
  8765 Runway Avenue
  Toronto, Ontario

  Pilot, with the responsibility for flying a DC-10 to major centres through-out North America.

July 1985 - July 1988: full-time employment

  Toronto Flying Club
  45 - 5th Avenue
  Toronto, Ontario

  Pilot/Flight Instructor for this company which provides chartered flight services to the general public, as well as comprehensive training in all aspects of commercial and private flight instruction.

BUSINESS REFERENCE

Mr. John Dolin, Managing Director
Airlines International Flight Centre
8765 Runway Avenue
Toronto, Ontario
Business telephone:(416) 963-1111

CHARACTER REFERENCE

Mr. Russel P. Crow, Retired B.O.A.C. Training Captain
123 Williams Crescent
Canberley, Surrey
United Kingdom
Home telephone: 0226-12345

RESUME #36
POLICE SERGEANT

Festus M. MacCloud
45 Constabulary Drive
Ottawa, Ontario
K1A 0C9

Home telephone: (819) 997-1058

PERSONAL INFORMATION

Birth date: March 24, 1948
Height: 5' 10"   Weight: 180 lbs.
Health: excellent

EDUCATIONAL BACKGROUND

Diploma (Grade 12): City Centre High School, Ottawa, Ontario, 1967

ADVANCED POLICE TRAINING (Provided Through The Canadian Police College)

- Advanced Police Science
- Surveillance Training
- Criminal Intelligence
- Media Relations Course
- Major Crime Investigation
- Interviewing & Interrogation Techniques

BASIC POLICE TRAINING

Basic Police Training, provided through the Ottawa City Police, Ottawa, Ontario, 1969

PROFESSIONAL INTEREST: reading LOSS AND PREVENTION MAGAZINE

AVAILABILITY: Minimum of one month's notice required.

PROFESSIONAL EXPERIENCE

April 1979 - present: full-time employment

  Ottawa City Police
  Ottawa, Ontario

<u>Sergeant</u> Reporting directly to the Staff Sergeant, principal duties and re-sponsibilities involve the following:

STAFF SUPERVISION: Responsible for supervising the activities of 26 regular members and one clerk stenographer (i.e., planning and scheduling of work-loads; assigning tasks; establishing priorities; ensuring staff compliance with directives, as well as updating policy and procedure manuals; etc.);

PUBLIC RELATIONS: Responsible for personally resolving inquiries or com-plaints from the general public in a polite and professional manner; provid-ing lectures and discussion groups on the role of the police within the com-munity, when required; responding to routine radio communications and inquiries over the Canada-wide computer network; participating in activities that help foster better relations between the police department and general community;

146

CRIMINAL INVESTIGATIONS: Responsible for supervising activities pertaining to criminal investigations (i.e., conspiracies to import narcotics into Canada; activities of major drug rings and seizure of illegal substances; homicides of civilians and fellow police officers; major vehicle theft rings; purchasing of stolen goods; armed robberies of financial institutions, as well as conspiracies to commit same, etc.); making recommendations to Crown Prosecutors on matters pertaining to criminal charges;

SECURITY: Responsible for ensuring the protection of the community and that the rights of prisoners are protected; keeping abreast of the various government statutes, acts and orders pertaining to the enforcement of the law (e.g., Court Procedures, Charges Information, Summonses, Warrants of Arrest, Search Warrants, Appearance Notices, Notice to Parents of Young Offenders, etc.); counselling representatives of the business community on how to create, develop and implement successful loss prevention programs in their businesses.

June 1969 - April 1979: full-time employment

Ontario Wholesalers Ltd.
4 Charlotte Street
Ottawa, Ontario

Director of Loss Prevention for this corporation's wholesale, retail and transportation operations that are located throughout Ontario. Responsible for securing and installing security systems and video equipment in the most effective locations of the corporation's premises; making the arrangements for the hiring of auxiliary personnel through local security companies, and supervising of same; conducting security checks of the corporation's various premises and audits of financial statements, as required.

BUSINESS REFERENCE

Mr. Garth Guardian, Chief of Police
Ottawa City Police
Ottawa, Ontario
Business telephone: (819) 997-1111

147

PRINCIPAL (COMMUNITY COLLEGE)

Gerald L. Comeau
222 Ivory Towers Drive
Toronto, Ontario
M7A 2H6

Home telephone: (416) 593-0000

PERSONAL INFORMATION

Birth date: April 18, 1953
Marital status: married   Number of Children: three
Health: excellent

EDUCATIONAL BACKGROUND

M.Ed. in School Administration: University of Toronto, Toronto, Ontario, 1985
B.Ed., University of Toronto: Toronto, Ontario, 1975
Diploma (Grade 12 Academic): Pearson High School, Toronto, Ontario, 1971

PRINCIPAL'S CERTIFICATE

Ontario Principal's Certificate, issued by the Department of Education, Province of Ontario, 1985

TEACHER'S LICENCE

Teacher's Licence, issued by the Department of Education, Province of Ontario, 1975

TEACHING CERTIFICATE

Teacher's Certificate 6, issued by the Department of Education, Province of Ontario, 1978

PROFESSIONAL ASSOCIATIONS

Canadian Vocational Association, active member from 1983 – present
Ontario Principals' Association, active member from 1983 – present
Ontario Association of Community College Administrators, active member from 1987 – present

PROFESSIONAL INTERESTS: keeping abreast of the ongoing publications in the field of education

SPECIAL RECOGNITION

Received the Ontario Order of Council Medallion Award in 1990 from the City of Toronto in recognition of outstanding contributions to the community

PROFESSIONAL EXPERIENCE

September 1975 – present

Toronto Community College
876 Pundit Road
Toronto, Ontario

Approximate Number of Department Heads:	35
Approximate Number of Full-time Staff:	300
Approximate Number of Full-time Students:	2,400
Approximate Number of Part-time Students:	7,000

Principal of this largest Community College within the Ontario Community College System.

[Promoted from the position of **Academic Instructor** (1975 – 1976) to **Adult Education Supervisor** (1976 – 1983) to **Acting Principal** (1983 – 1987) to the position of **Principal** (1987 – present)]. Reporting directly to the Assistant Deputy Minister on educational objectives and results, principal duties and responsibilities involve the following:
Staff Supervision: Responsible for directing the activities of teachers, department heads, maintenance personnel, food service staff, clerical and accounting staff, student services personnel, stores and purchasing staff, security and safety personnel, public relations and audio-visual personnel; promoting a team approach in the implementation and management of the educational goals, objectives and processes of the College;

Administrating The College's $32 Million Budget: Responsible for administrating the College's $32 Million budget; preparing budget profiles (i.e., detailed descriptions of the College's aims and objectives and financial needs for continued government funding);

Conducting And/Or Arranging In-Service Educational Programs: Responsible for conducting in-service educational programs and/or making the necessary arrangements for having qualified resource people speak on topics which may be of benefit to the entire staff;

Public Relations: Responsible for personally resolving in a polite and professional manner inquiries and/or complaints from the general public, in person or over the telephone; determining the need for new programming in the College through interviews and consultations with representatives of public and private agencies; promoting effective relations between the College and general public by participating in various community events and activities;

Personnel Administration: Responsible for chairing group hiring decisions; preparing financial forecasts on the short and long term personnel requirements of the College; administrating collective agreements; conducting Performance Evaluations.

<u>Extracurricular Activities</u>:

1. Served as a Chairperson of the Student-Staff Liaison Committee from 1980 – 1985;

2. Served as a Supervisor of student social and recreational activities from 1978 – 1980;

3. Served as President of the Staff Association from 1975 – 1980.

<u>Special Educational Projects</u>:

1. Between 1980 – 1982, created a Department of Student Services, which has since served as a model for all Campuses in the Ontario Community College System. The services to students provided by this Department are as follows: a Canada Manpower Center; a Professional Student Counsellor; Computerized Student Records; a College

Program Marketing Department; a Scholarship Program; and Student Health Services;

2. Between 1978 – 1980, organized and implemented a restructuring of the following College components: Campus Administration; Stores and Accounting; Plant Maintenance; Student Services; and Media Services;

3. Between 1975 – 1978, served as a Chairperson of several Curriculum Development Committees at both Campus and Provincial levels.

Special Mandate: In 1991, personally visited the Campuses of Community Colleges located in British Columbia, Alberta, and the Maritime Provinces, in order to: **1.** directly observe their facilities; **2.** have general discussions with their several representatives on the types of educational programs and services provided by their respective Colleges; and **3.** discuss, in particular, matters pertaining to college administration and student services.

BUSINESS AND CHARACTER REFERENCES: Available Upon Request.

RESUME #38
PROGRAM COORDINATOR

Penelope G. Planner
45 Development Street
Hartford, CT 06106

Home telephone: (203) 566-0011

PERSONAL INFORMATION

Birth date: January 26, 1947

EDUCATIONAL BACKGROUND

Bachelor of Public Relations: Saint Mary's University, Hartford, Connecticut, 1969

Diploma (Grade 12 Academic): Beth High School, Hartford, Connecticut, 1965

SPECIAL SKILLS AND ABILITIES

- Possess strong interpersonal communication skills, and have a demonstrated interest in working harmoniously with others
- Have strong organizing, managing, and motivating skills

AVAILABILITY: Immediate.

SALARY EXPECTED: Open — nature and challenge of position itself is of principal concern.

PROFESSIONAL EXPERIENCE

September 1976 - October 1991: full-time employment
 Connecticut Department of Agriculture & Rural Development
 P.O. Box 54
 Hartford, Connecticut

Program Coordinator for this non-profit organization whose goal is to foster leadership and interpersonal communication skills in youths through active participation in its educational and recreational programs.

Reporting directly to the Board of Directors on program objectives and results, principal duties and responsibilities involved the following:

Setting Up Programs: Responsible for setting up programs on leader-ship training and development (i.e., Personal Goal Setting, Life Skills, Self-Esteem Development, Coping With Peer Pressure, etc.).
{Specific contributions on these programs involved the following: formulating the description of proposed programs and outline of specific aims and objectives; forecasting costs of programs and probable impact on the membership; determining space, special equipment and facilities needed; formulating the time schedules; establishing essential records and recording procedures; arranging for special guest speakers; determining the means for programs to be continued on a self-supporting basis; determining methods of program evaluation};

Arranging Publicity: Responsible for promoting public awareness of available programs through effective advertising campaigns (i.e., creating and developing information packages to advertise the availability of the programs to the general public; preparing media kits and press releases; maintaining a bank of information on the times, dates, and locations of planned events; preparing slide shows, audio/video presentations, and lectures);

Fund Raising & Administrating Program Budgets: Responsible for organizing and implementing fund raising campaigns, as well as acting as a liaison between the organization and its corporate sponsors; preparing budget profiles (i.e., detailed descriptions of the organization's aims and objectives and financial needs for continued government and corporate funding); controlling, developing and evaluating all phases of financial reporting;

Recruiting & Training Of Volunteers: Responsible for recruiting, training, and supervising as many as seventy volunteers (i.e., interpreting policies and procedures issued from top management; coaching volunteers through all aspects of their responsibilities; conducting follow-ups to ensure that assignments are properly completed; promoting a team approach to problem solving, etc.).

June 1969 – September 1976: full-time employment
Eastern Paper
Wentworth Street
Hartford, Connecticut

Sales Desk Operator for this company which specializes in the sale and distribution of paper products.

BUSINESS AND CHARACTER REFERENCES: Available Upon Request.

Irene Q. Aptitude
345 Counsel Drive
Toronto, Ontario
M7A 2H6

Home telephone: (416) 963-0387

PERSONAL INFORMATION

Birth date: January 23, 1956
Marital status: married   Dependents: three

EDUCATIONAL BACKGROUND

M.A. in Psychology, University of Toronto, Toronto, Ontario, 1979
  Thesis: "A Study to Determine if the Ego is Changed Measurably as a Result
  of Closed Environment Exposure."

Scholarship: Graduate Assistantship — Assistant to Dean of Students
  B.A. in Psychology (magna cum laude), University of Toronto, Toronto, Ontario, 1977

Diploma (Grade 12 Academic): Pearson Senior High School, Toronto, Ontario, 1973
  Graduated With Honors

PUBLICATIONS

Edited A Specific, Integrated Model For Selecting Provincial Assessment Objectives, which was prepared for the Ontario Board of Education, October 1987

Author of Analysis On Staffing Adjustments At Toronto City Hospital, which was prepared for the Ontario Mental Health Association, October 1978

PROFESSIONAL AFFILIATION

Ontario Association of Psychologists, interim member since 1979

PROFESSIONAL EXPERIENCE

September 5, 1983 - present: full-time employment
  Ontario Penitentiary
  P.O. Box 2140
  Toronto, Ontario

Psychologist for this medium security federal government penitentiary which has approximately 475 male inmates serving sentences ranging from two years to life imprisonment.

Reporting directly to the Coordinator of the Psychology Department, principal duties and responsibilities involve the following:

Counseling: Responsible for assessing the needs of offenders at any given time in their sentence (i.e., mental, emotional, physical, social); investigating the psycho-social histories of offenders within the institution in order to facilitate more purposeful communication during counselling sessions; discussing and resolving problems with inmates, with respect and dignity shown at all times to those concerned, regardless of their type of offence or ethnic background; providing group training in the areas of self-esteem development and coping with peer pressure;

Conducting Mental Status Reviews: Responsible for conducting mental status assessments of offenders through individual testing, clinical interviews, case history examination, and institutional performance, in order to determine: **1**. their risk of psychological breakdown, **2**. risk of suicide, **3**. risk of danger to staff or other inmates, **4**. risk of danger to the community (and probability of recidivism in regards to transfers, temporary absences, and parole), and **5**. need for psychiatric referral; recommending appropriate treatment or programs for inmates based upon the findings and conclusions of these assessments concerning their personality, mental status, and cognitive, educational, and vocational abilities;

Administrating Psychological Tests: Responsible for administrating, scoring and evaluating individual psychological tests (primarily MMPI) for offenders; providing testimony in courtroom jury trials as an expert witness on the psychometric testing of defendants.

July 1979 – July 1983: full-time employment
Child Care and Development Branch
1234 Enlightenment Road
Toronto, Ontario

School Psychologist: Reporting directly to Regional Coordinator, principal duties and responsibilities involved conducting psycho-logical and educational evaluations; administrating, scoring, and writing evaluations of psychological tests for students which include testing in the areas of ability, achievement, giftedness, aptitude, emotional stability, and personality traits; general counselling of students and/or parents; counselling students on problems pertaining to their home environment, social skills, and behavioral problems.

BUSINESS AND CHARACTER REFERENCES: Available Upon Request.

RESUME #40
REAL ESTATE SALES REPRESENTATIVE

Joseph S. Property
17 Commercial Lane
Providence, RI 02903

Home telephone: (401) 277-3333

EDUCATIONAL BACKGROUND

Fellow of the Real Estate Institute of Appraisals (F.R.I.): taken through the
University of Rhode Island, Providence, Rhode Island, 1982

Diploma (Grade 12 Academic): Grant High School, Providence, Rhode Island, 1971

REAL ESTATE LICENSES

Brokers' License, issued through the Providence Real Estate Council, Providence, Rhode Island, 1973

Real Estate Sales' License, issued through the Providence Real Estate Council,
Providence, Rhode Island, 1971

PROFESSIONAL AFFILIATIONS

Member in good standing of the United States Real Estate Association since 1971
Member in good standing of the Providence Real Estate Board since 1971

SPECIAL SKILLS AND ABILITIES

- Possess strong negotiating and interpersonal communication skills, and have
  a demonstrated interest in working harmoniously with others
- Can organize own personal time and tasks efficiently
- Can present a professional company image to clients, fellow workers, and/or
  peers

BUSINESS EXPERIENCE

April 1980 - present: full-time employment
  Central Real Estate Ltd.
  777 Endowment Road
  Providence, Rhode Island

Real Estate Sales Agent for this real estate company which specializes in
the sale of residential, commercial and industrial real estate, and real estate appraisals. Reporting directly to the President, principal duties and
responsibilities involve the following:

Real Estate Sales: Responsible for formulating sales strategy and direction
(e.g., market development, major account sales activities, etc.); drafting
and presenting proposals to clients which emphasize the selling points and
benefits of real estate handled by the company; negotiating compromises and
preparing legally binding agreements between buyers and sellers, under the
Real Estate Act of Rhode Island; making property appraisals through both comparative and cost approaches; ensuring that all transactions are in accordance with state government statutes and policies; keeping informed and advising clients on market trends and trading strategies;

Land Use Development: Responsible for bringing purchasers into joint venture agreements to purchase and develop raw land or upgrade existing building utilization and income; renegotiating leases and rents; developing analyses of land use projection concerned with proposed incomes, expenses and cost to achieve desired results, as well as obtaining the preliminary plans, permits, zoning modifications and reclassifications to assist in the development of land or resale of land for proposed use; acting on the behalf of buyers for the purpose of securing parcels of land;

Acting As a Liaison: Responsible for acting as a liaison between clients and lawyers on the following matters: **a**) Title Clearings; **b**) Advancement of Funds; **c**) Foreclosures; and **d**) Acquiring and Selling Properties.

Special Sales Achievements: In 1988, 1989, and 1990, received the Real Estate Agent Of The Year Award in recognition of outstanding sales achievements.

June 1971 - April 1980: full-time employment

Big Sale Realty Ltd.
23 Century Drive
Providence, Rhode Island

Real Estate Agent for this company which specializes in the sale of residential, commercial and industrial real estate.
Special Sales Achievements: Received numerous awards throughout my career with this company in recognition of top sales achievements.

BUSINESS REFERENCES: Available Upon Request.

Kathleen H. Gourmet
555 Kent Street
Charlottetown, Prince Edward Island
C1A 7N8

Home telephone: (902) 892-1111

EDUCATIONAL BACKGROUND

Food Services Management & Personnel Administration Program: Holland College,
  Charlottetown, Prince Edward Island, 1980
  Diploma (Grade 12 Academic): Dr. Grey High School, Toronto, Ontario, 1978

SPECIAL SKILLS AND ABILITIES

• Can plan workloads and supervise subordinates to the best advantage
• Can present a professional company image to the general public, fellow workers, subordinates and/or peers

PROFESSIONAL INTERESTS: reading the CANADIAN RESTAURANT MAGAZINE; gourmet cook-
  ing

BUSINESS EXPERIENCE

June 1985 - January 1991: full-time employment

  English Steak & Seafood Restaurant
  63 St. George Street
  Charlottetown, Prince Edward Island

  Approximate Seating Capacity:125
  Number of Employees Personally Responsible For:15
  Average Number of Hours Worked (per week):55 - 60

Manager of this fully licensed restaurant which features steak and seafood
menu items. Reporting directly to the Board of Directors on business objectives and results, principal duties and responsibilities involved the following:

PUBLIC RELATIONS: Responsible for receiving customer payments in cash and/or
credit card; handling the inquiries and/or complaints of customers, over the
telephone or in person, in a polite and professional manner; promoting public awareness of the restaurant through good customer service;

STAFF SUPERVISION: Responsible for supervising the activities of cashiers,
waitresses, bartenders, hostesses, floor managers, kitchen staff and chefs
(i.e., planning and scheduling of workloads; assigning tasks; establishing
priorities; promoting a working environment that is conducive to greater
learning and involvement, in order to ensure a minimum turnover of staff; ensuring that company policies respecting matters of restaurant security are
strictly adhered to);

COORDINATING SPECIAL FUNCTIONS: Responsible for determining staffing and supervisory requirements for special functions such as business luncheons,
tour groups and weddings, etc.; coordinating reservations in order to
achieve maximum volume; maintaining sales records;

INVENTORY CONTROL: Responsible for requisitioning, issuing and controlling inventory on all perishable and nonperishable supplies; certifying all invoices pertaining to food, liquor and beverages, and submitting statements of such same to the Accountant;

STAFF TRAINING: Responsible for providing basic training to newly hired employees (i.e., interpreting the restaurant's policies and procedures to new recruits on matters pertaining to good customer service and neat housekeeping standards; coaching new employees through all aspects of their responsibilities; providing adequate motivation to new employees in order to ensure their abilities are fully utilized; ensuring that all staff members are properly instructed in the restaurant's policies pertaining to codes of professional conduct and dress, etc.).

June 1980 - June 1985: full-time employment

Weymouth Diner
52 Weymouth Street
Charlottetown, Prince Edward Island

Cook for this restaurant which features Canadian food menu items. Principal duties and responsibilities involved the following:

PREPARING A WIDE VARIETY OF FOOD MENU ITEMS: Responsible for preparing roast turkey dinners for banquets, hot and cold buffets, sandwiches, and other requested food menu items;

ENSURING QUALITY CONTROL: Responsible for ensuring adherence to sound professional practices in the preparation of all food menu items, and that all aspects of proper sanitation methods and procedures were strictly complied with.

RESUME #42
SALES MANAGER (ADVERTISING)

Daniel S. Tout
82 Proclamation Drive
Ottawa, Ontario
K1A 0C9

Home telephone: (819) 997-2222

PERSONAL INFORMATION

Birth date: June 5, 1959
Health: excellent

EDUCATIONAL BACKGROUND

Bachelor of Public Relations: University of Ottawa, Ottawa, Ontario, 1981
  Area of concentration: Advertising and Marketing
  Diploma (Grade 12 Academic): Derrick Senior High School, Ottawa, Ontario,
  1977

AVAILABILITY: Immediate.

SALARY EXPECTED: Open — nature and challenge of position itself is of principal concern.

BUSINESS EXPERIENCE

May 1981 - January 1992

  Flyer Delivery Inc.
  123 1st Avenue
  Ottawa, Ontario

Advertising Manager of this company which publishes an advertising flyer
that has a weekly circulation of 380,000 throughout the Ottawa area.

Reporting directly to the President on business objectives and results, principal duties and responsibilities involved the following:

Staff Supervision: Responsible for supervising the activities of thirteen
Sales Representatives, one Distribution Manager, four Secretaries and nine
warehouse employees (i.e., planning and scheduling of workloads; assigning
tasks; establishing priorities; providing adequate motivation in order to ensure their abilities are fully utilized; etc.);

Client Relations: Responsible for meeting with representatives of the
company's clients on a regular basis in order to discuss the types of advertising services that their operations need to help meet their business
needs; personally resolving their inquiries or complaints in a professional
and courteous manner; processing customer orders; promoting public awareness
of the company through good client service;

Marketing: Responsible for managing all phases of the company's Advertising
Flyer in order to ensure a maximization of profit in the company (i.e., formulating sales strategy and direction; establishing sales targets, market development, major account sales activities, industry profiles, etc.); drafting and presenting sales proposals which emphasize the selling points and

benefits of company services to prospective clients; interpreting the significance of FAS-FAX statistics issued from ABC (the Audit Bureau of Circulation) in order to demonstrate to clients the dollar value of their advertising fees against advertising fees in other types of media (i.e., cost per thousand and cost per rating point);

Market Research: Responsible for collecting demographic statistics for market research projects (i.e., general data for direct mailings to home owners and businesses; collecting data from such sources as municipal, provincial and federal government agencies, etc.); conducting follow-up surveys with customers in order to obtain research information on their satisfaction or dissatisfaction with company services;

Developing Pricing, Rating & Route Structures: Responsible for organizing and implementing an interline network which upon completion would complement existing delivery services provided by the company (i.e., developing profitable pricing, rating and route structures);

Training New Sales Representatives: Responsible for coaching new recruits through all aspects of their sales (i.e., sales approach, answering sales objections, sales analysis, closing sales, and active sales presentations).

BUSINESS REFERENCE

Mr. William Press, President
Budget Flyer Delivery Inc.
Flyer Delivery Inc.
123 1st Avenue
Ottawa, Ontario
Business telephone: (819) 997-1111

RESUME #43
SALES REPRESENTATIVE

Catherine E. Price
49 Executive Drive
Jackson, MS 39201

Home telephone: (601) 359-5555

PERSONAL INFORMATION

Birth date: May 9, 1955
Marital status: married   Dependents: two

EDUCATIONAL BACKGROUND

Diploma (Grade 12 Academic): Jackson High School, Jackson, Mississippi, 1973

SPECIAL SKILLS AND ABILITIES

- Enjoy challenges, and work with enthusiasm and high energy on all assignments
- Can present a professional company image to clients, fellow workers, and/or peers

TRAVEL: Willing to comply with all travelling requirements.

PROFESSIONAL INTERESTS: reading business journals on marketing and finance

HOBBIES AND INTERESTS: meeting people, baseball, golf, and nutrition

AVAILABILITY: Minimum of two weeks' notice required.

SALARY EXPECTED: Negotiable.

SALES EXPERIENCE

November 1973 - present: full-time employment
  Elegant Furniture Co. Ltd.
  317 Bonne Street
  Jackson, Mississippi

Sales Representative for this national company which specializes in the manufacturing and sale of furniture to retail operations.

[Promoted from the position of **Shipper Receiver** to **Inside Sales Person** to **Sales Representative**]

Reporting directly to the Sales Manager on business objectives and results, with a commission sales territory covering the State of Mississippi, principal duties and responsibilities involve the following:

Client Relations: Responsible for servicing approximately 70 independent accounts, among which include Eaten's Ltd., Hudson River Co. and Seers; selling medium to high-end quality furniture; conducting interviews with the representatives of dealers on matters pertaining to the types of furniture and/or services that their operations need to help meet their business needs; personally resolving inquiries or complaints from clients in a professional and courteous manner (i.e., on matters pertaining to sales, lost goods, damages, returns, holds for pick-ups, present locality of shipments, order processing, etc.); promoting public awareness of the company through good client service;

Marketing: Responsible for formulating sales strategy and direction (e.g., market development, major account sales activities, industry profiles, pricing, etc.); drafting and presenting proposals which emphasize the selling points and benefits of company products and services to prospective clients; representing the company at Trade Shows and Market Places in order to introduce new and existing product lines;

Sales Analysis: Responsible for balancing sales receipts on a weekly basis, as well as forwarding a record of such receipts to Head Office; ensuring that all financial transactions are properly authorized and in accordance with company policies, as well as taking corrective measures on any irregularities; preparing periodic and special reports to determine the viability and competitiveness of the company within its sales territory (e.g., Quarterly Fiscal Year Sales Comparisons and Quarterly Net Sales Comparisons);

Out-Of-Town Business Trips: Responsible for maintaining personal records of expenditure on out-of-town business trips (e.g., time sheets, mileage, hotel and meal expenses, etc.), as well as arranging own itineraries on this eight week cycle.

Special Sales Achievements: Since the outset of my sales career with this company, I have been acknowledged on numerous occasions for above average ranking in the placement of new accounts and for the highest percentage increase in quota sales in six product categories.

Note: This position requires an ability to work with confidence, accuracy, efficiency, and understanding under all types of pressure situations; and throughout my employment, I have played a key role in making recommendations that have facilitated better client service, an improved workflow, and better staff relations. I have also consistently scored high on all Performance Evaluations conducted by the company.

BUSINESS REFERENCES: Available Upon Request.

RESUME #44
INSURANCE SALES REPRESENTATIVE

Yvon S. Warranty
268 Coverage Road
Vancouver, British Columbia
V8W 3E6

Home telephone: (604) 387-5101

EDUCATIONAL BACKGROUND

Life Underwriter's Association of Canada Training Program: sponsored by Insurance of Canada Ltd., Vancouver, British Columbia, 1971

Diploma (Grade 12): Grey High School, Vancouver, British Columbia, 1969

PROFESSIONAL EXPERIENCE

July 1970 - present: full-time employment
   Insurance of Canada Ltd.
   123 Hastings Street
   Vancouver, British Columbia

Group Marketing Consultant for this national insurance company.
Specific responsibilities involve the following:
Sales Promotion: Responsible for selling personal life, disability, medical, home, and automobile insurance, as well as pensions and mutual funds; drafting and presenting proposals which emphasize the selling points and benefits of the company's financial products and services to prospective clients; providing consultation services to union leaders on group insurance plans and employee benefits available through cost shared agreements, as well as occasionally assisting on the negotiations of such benefits; counselling company clients on such matters as tax deferral plans and portfolio management; providing consultation services on pensions and group insurance products.

June 1969 - July 1970: full-time employment

   Hillside Estates Ltd.
   678 Granville Street
   Vancouver, British Columbia

Sales Representative for this company which specializes in the sale of mobile and mini-homes.

BUSINESS REFERENCES: Available Upon Request.

RESUME #45
SALES REPRESENTATIVE (NEW & USED CARS)

Jeffrey F. Car
123 1st Avenue
Toronto, Ontario
M7A 2H6

Home telephone: (416) 596-0000

EDUCATIONAL BACKGROUND

Diploma (Grade 12 Academic): Wentworth High School, Toronto, Ontario, 1976

AVAILABILITY: Minimum of two weeks' notice required.

SALARY EXPECTED: Open — nature and challenge of position itself is of principal concern.

BUSINESS EXPERIENCE

March 1976 - present

The Automotive Ltd.
689 12th Avenue
Toronto, Ontario

Sales Representative for this automobile dealership which specializes in the sale of new and used cars. Principal duties and responsibilities involve the following:

Automobile Sales & Appraisals: Responsible for drafting and presenting sales proposals which emphasize the selling points and benefits of company vehicles and services to prospective clients, as well as personally closing 50% of all deals for the company; conducting appraisals on all trade-ins for the company; making the necessary arrangements for detailing on used cars (i.e., mechanical and body work, damage repairs, metal replacements, painting, etc.); verifying documentation concerned with transfer of ownership and insurance; arranging financing for customers through Chartered Banks and Trust Companies; developing and maintaining good working relationships with the representatives of Chartered Banks and Trust Companies on matters pertaining to sold cars; conducting follow-up surveys with customers in order to obtain research information on their satisfaction or dissatisfaction with company services and/or products.

BUSINESS AND CHARACTER REFERENCES: Available Upon Request.

RESUME #46
SCHOOL TEACHER

Pamela D. Pundit
63 Acumen Crescent
Vancouver, British Columbia
V8W 3E6

Home telephone: (604) 387-5555

PERSONAL INFORMATION

Birth date: May 25, 1955
Marital status: single   Dependents: none

EDUCATIONAL BACKGROUND

M.Ed. in School Administration University of British Columbia, Vancouver, British Columbia, 1980

B.Ed. in Secondary Social Studies, University of Victoria, Victoria, British Columbia, 1977

Diploma (Grade 12 Academic): Vancouver High School, Vancouver, British Columbia, 1973

TEACHING CERTIFICATE

Teacher's Certificate 5, issued by the Department of Education, Province of British Columbia, 1980

PROFESSIONAL ASSOCIATION

British Columbia Teachers' Association, member since 1980

EDUCATIONAL WORKSHOPS AND SEMINARS ATTENDED

Have attended numerous educational workshops and seminars provided by the British Columbia Teachers' Union since the outset of my teaching career.

TEACHING EXPERIENCE

September 1980 - present: full-time employment

    School District #15
    Vancouver City School
    256 Granville Street
    Vancouver, British Columbia

School Teacher: Principal duties and responsibilities involve the following:

Teaching: Responsible for teaching all subjects, excluding French, to students enrolled in grade ten, eleven, and twelve, in accordance with the philosophy of School District #15; providing adequate motivation to students in order to ensure their abilities on assigned tasks are fully developed and utilized; conducting oral interviews on work covered, when required; fostering a classroom environment that encourages greater learning and involvement among all students;

School Discipline: Responsible for the day-to-day discipline of students, when necessary (i.e., discussing and resolving disciplinary problems with students, staff, parents, and pupil personnel staff, with respect and dignity shown at all times to those concerned, regardless of their socio-economic or ethnic background);

Public Relations: Responsible for personally resolving in a polite and professional manner inquiries, concerns, and/or complaints from the parents of students, in person or over the telephone; conducting parent/teacher interviews; promoting effective relations between the school and general public by participating in various community events and activities;

Attending Staff Meetings: Responsible for attending staff meetings in order to: **1.** acquire information on the availability of any recently updated educational material; **2.** provide input on the types of special in-service educational programs that may be introduced to help meet teaching needs; **3.** evaluate the merits of past achievements; **4.** establish new priorities; **5.** integrate the collection of information and tasks; **6.** facilitate a normal and efficient work-flow; and **7.** keep abreast of any changes in school board policy and procedure.

Extracurricular Activities:
1. Supervise school dances and other recreational activities
2. Participate on the school's Winter Carnival Committee
3. Participate on Student Council, Student Fund Raising Campaigns, and Home & School

BUSINESS AND CHARACTER REFERENCES: Available Upon Request.

EXECUTIVE SECRETARY

Patricia C. Calendar
123 5th Avenue
Los Angeles, CA 95814

Home telephone: (916) 324-1111

EDUCATIONAL BACKGROUND

Secretarial & Accounting Diploma Program: Los Angeles Business College, Los Angeles, California, 1973
Diploma (Grade 12 Academic): Royal High School, Los Angeles, California, 1971

SPECIAL SKILLS AND ABILITIES

- Possess strong interpersonal communication skills, and have a demonstrated interest in working harmoniously with others
- Have a strong knowledge of office practice and procedure
- Can present a professional company image to clients, fellow workers, subordinates and/or peers

BUSINESS EXPERIENCE

February 1980 – present: full-time employment
  Frozen Foods Canada Ltd.
  243 Commercial Avenue
  Los Angeles, California

Executive Secretary for this international company which specializes in the sale of canned and frozen food products.

Reporting directly to the President and Vice President on business objectives and results, principal duties and responsibilities involve the following:

Public Relations: Responsible for answering and screening telephone calls for the Vice President and other staff members in a polite and professional manner; maintaining a calendar of appointments and meetings for the Vice President, as well as preparing and assembling data and background documents that are required for such meetings; receiving and directing individuals to the appropriate personnel; promoting public awareness of the company through good customer service;

Regional Liaison Duties: Responsible for acting as a liaison between the company's head office and its regional offices in Los Angeles, Manhattan Beach and San Jose for the purpose of discussing and resolving day-to-day routine office administrative problems;

Office Administration: Responsible for preparing periodic and special reports on key accounts to determine the viability and competitiveness of the company against previous years (e.g., Fiscal Year Sales Comparisons and Net Sales Comparisons); ordering, issuing, and controlling inventory on all office supplies and business equipment, as well as preparing budget forecasts on future needs; receiving and perusing all incoming mail, as well as redirecting it to appropriate staff members for action; ensuring that all filing systems are properly maintained; updating the company's policies and procedures manual, as required; typing and composing of letters and memos for signature, with the responsibility for their correct grammar, spelling and punctuation; transcribing and typing minutes of meetings, memos, reports, statements, etc. from written notes or verbal instructions;

Computer Applications: Responsible for using WordPerfect (5.1), Lotus 1-2-3, Graphics Gallery, HP DESK (Electronic Mail), Advance-write Plus and an AccPac/Bedford computerized integrated ccounting system which includes accounts payable/receivable, general ledger, payroll, and job costing; operating an on-line computerized information retrieval system, as well as analyzing and interpreting data from it;

Arranging Out-of-Town Business Trips: Responsible for setting up, on an ongoing basis, the travel arrangements for company personnel on out-of-town business assignments (e.g., contacting travel agencies; booking airfares; arranging for hotel accommodations and automobile rentals; handling advances and claims; arranging business itineraries; etc.).

June 1973 – February 1980: full-time employment
    The Stationer Limited
    89 Staple Road
    Los Angeles, California

Accounts Receivable Clerk for this company which specializes in the sale of business machines and miscellaneous stationery supplies.

BUSINESS AND CHARACTER REFERENCES: Available Upon Request.

RESUME #48
SHIP NAVIGATION (LEADING SEAMAN)

Jake C. Bly
45 River Road
Sacramento, CA 95814

Home telephone: (916) 324-1111

PERSONAL INFORMATION

Birth date: March 18, 1968
Health: excellent
Physical handicaps: none
Passport: Have a valid passport.

EDUCATIONAL BACKGROUND

Watchkeeping Mate Certificate: Navigation Community College, Sacramento, California, 1989 - 1990

Areas of concentration:
- Navigating Instruments and SEN 1 (Radar)- Chartwork & Pilotage
- General Ship Knowledge- Navigational Safety
- General Seamanship

Diploma (Grade 12 Academic): Sacramento High School, Sacramento, California, 1989

SPECIAL SKILLS AND ABILITIES

- Possess strong interpersonal communication skills, and have a demonstrated interest in working harmoniously with others
- Can present a professional company image to clients, fellow workers, subordinates and/or peers

AVAILABILITY: Two weeks' notice required.

PROFESSIONAL EXPERIENCE

January 1990 - present: permanent relief work
  Motor Vessel M. Vanacos
  1801 Palm Beach Road
  Sacramento, CA

Leading Seaman working on this American-owned petroleum tanker which sails the coast of Chile through the Straits of Magellan to the Begal Channel. Reporting directly to the Chief Officer, principal duties and responsibilities involve the following:

Steering the Vessel: Responsible for steering the ship, as well as giving the appropriate responses to the Captain and/or Chief Officer; learning the effect of propellers and rudder on steering; acquiring a practical knowledge of leading marks and lines, transits, sector lights, and lines of bearing; calculating times and heights of high and low water at reference and secondary ports, as well as calculating the depth of waters at those times, in cooperation with other employees;

General Seamanship Duties: Responsible for observing weather conditions; rigging the ship; doing basic knotting, gripping and splicing, with reference to current practices, seizings, rackings, and stoppers; reeving of blocks and purchases; rigging of stages and chairs; organizing and doing routine bridge discipline, under all types of circumstances and weather conditions; tending of lines and gangways; conducting routine fire patrols and inspections; observing safety precautions when taking on or transferring fuel, water, stores and/or materials; assuming anchor watch duties and responsibilities; acquiring a working knowledge of line-throwing appliances, including aiming and firing; caring and stowage of life boat equipment and drinking water; acquiring a practical knowledge of general maneuvering characteristics and of the lifesaving signals; acquiring a working knowledge of the duties and responsibilities of the master, officer of the watch, pilot and other bridge personnel (jointly and separately), as well as the purpose, necessity and general content of standing orders, night orders, bridge or movement book, and ship's log book;

General Ship Knowledge: Responsible for acquiring a working knowledge of general ship construction, including knowledge of framing, shell plating, decks, water-tight bulkheads, hatchways, bilges, double-bottoms, sounding pipes and air pipes; reading draft and finding mean drafts;

Navigational Safety: Responsible for practicing good housekeeping standards, in order to ensure the occupational health and safety of all employees; keeping abreast of Collision Regulations, Rules of the Road, and Recommended Code of Navigation Practices and Procedures; acquiring a practical working knowledge of pollution prevention regulations and practices as defined in the Oil Pollution Prevention Regulations, Garbage Pollution Prevention Regulations, and Shipping Safety Control Zones Order.

BUSINESS AND CHARACTER REFERENCES: Available Upon Request.

RESUME #49
SOCIAL WORKER

Norman R. Welfare
96 Wimbley Court
Lincoln, NE 68509

Home telephone: (402) 471-2222
Business telephone: (402) 471-1111

PERSONAL INFORMATION

Birth date: June 28, 1960
Marital status: single   Dependents: none
Health: excellent

EDUCATIONAL BACKGROUND

Bachelor of Social Work: University of Nebraska, Lincoln, Nebraska, 1983

B.A., University of Nebraska, Lincoln, Nebraska, 1981
  Major: Community Studies

Diploma (Grade 12 Academic): Morrison High School, Lincoln, Nebraska, 1978

WORKSHOPS AND SEMINARS ATTENDED

"Sexual Abuse Investigations Course," sponsored by the State Department of Justice and Health and Community Services, Lincoln, Nebraska, 1987
  Duration: two weeks

"Training & Family Therapy," sponsored by the United States Health and Community Services, Lincoln, Nebraska, 1987
  Duration: sixty hours of intensive training

SPECIAL SKILLS AND ABILITIES

- Possess strong interpersonal communication skills, and have a demonstrated interest in working harmoniously with others
- Can present a professional company image to clients, fellow workers, subordinates and/or peers

HOBBIES AND INTERESTS: meeting people; reading literature; physical fitness; volunteer work with seniors and children; creative writing

AVAILABILITY: Minimum of two weeks' notice required.

SALARY EXPECTED: Open — nature and challenge of position itself is of principal concern.

PROFESSIONAL EXPERIENCE

June 1983 - present: full-time employment
  Department of Health and Community Services
  P.O. Box 6987
  Lincoln, Nebraska

Child Protection Worker
Reporting directly to the Unit Supervisor, and acting under the appropriate legal authority designated by the State Department of Social Services, principal duties and responsibilities involve the following:

CHILD ABUSE INVESTIGATIONS: Responsible for investigating cases of actual and/or potential child neglect, abuse, and sexual assault, as well as providing child welfare intervention services where appropriate, in accordance with the Family Services Act; attending family court proceedings for the purpose of filing applications and providing necessary evidence concerning apprehended children;

CRISIS INTERVENTION: Responsible for providing on-the-scene emergency social intervention services (e.g., providing on-the-scene assistance to the police and family members regarding lost or found children, as well as assisting with all intermediate activities related to cases of delinquency or during domestic disputes; providing crisis intervention services on attempted suicides and for individuals experiencing severe emotional and/or psychiatric problems (e.g., social assessments, short and long-term treatment undertakings, etc.);

CHILD PROTECTION SERVICES: Responsible for making the necessary arrangements for the care, custody, discipline, and rehabilitation of assigned youths; orienting children to available community resources;

COUNSELING: Responsible for providing crisis counseling services to a generic caseload (e.g., single parent families; the emotionally disturbed; drug, solvent and alcohol abusers; children with behavioral problems, etc.); conducting home visitations; observing the interpersonal relationships between parents and their children; establishing long and short term goals to enhance the capabilities of children in conjunction with parents, school administrators, and other helping professionals; keeping informed and advising clients on the Family Services Act.

BUSINESS AND CHARACTER REFERENCES: Available Upon Request.

RESUME #50
STATIONARY ENGINEER

Patrick E. Plant
135 Mecca Drive
Regina, Saskatchewan
S4P 3V7

Home telephone: (306) 565-2970

EDUCATIONAL BACKGROUND

Stationary Engineer (Class III): taken through the Saskatchewan Community College (Regina Campus), Regina, Saskatchewan, 1983

Diploma (Grade 12 Industrial): James D. Memorial High School, Regina, Saskatchewan, 1979

PROFESSIONAL EXPERIENCE

September 1989 - present: full-time employment
  Regina Hospital
  (Supply Department)
  Regina, Saskatchewan

Stationary Engineer: Duties and responsibilities involve maintaining a safe and efficient operation of a steam generation plant (e.g., troubleshooting and diagnosing mechanical and electrical malfunctions); chemical analysis and treatment of feed water; analyzing flue gases to determine effective combustion of fuels, as well as taking any appropriate corrective measures.

May 1985 - September 1989: full-time employment
  Regina Radar Base
  Regina, Saskatchewan

Labourer: Duties and responsibilities involved performing general maintenance duties on the base's roads and grounds.

May 1983 - May 1985: full-time employment
  CFB Regina
  (Air Force Base)
  Regina, Saskatchewan

Labourer: Duties and responsibilities involved assisting tradespeople on various projects (i.e., plumbing and warehouse construction); maintaining grounds and roads.

BUSINESS REFERENCES: Available Upon Request.

RESUME #51
STUDENT

Sara H. Novice
322 Main Street
Carson City, NV 89710

Home telephone: (702) 885-5555

PERSONAL INFORMATION

Birth date: November 28, 1969
Health: excellent
Citizenship: American
Social Security Number: 321-21-4321
Nevada drivers' license number: EPA123456

EDUCATIONAL BACKGROUND

B.A., University of Nevada, Carson City, Nevada, 1991
  Major: Sociology
  Minor: Political Science
  Extracurricular Activities:
  1.From 1990 - 1991, served as Chairperson of the Student Representative
  Council
  2.From 1989 - 1990, served as a Student Representative at General Faculty
  Meetings
Diploma (Grade 12 Academic): Grey High School, Carson City, Nevada, 1987
  Special Recognition: Received the All Year Round Student Award for outstand-
  ing contributions of talents and energies to various academic, social and ex-
  tracurricular activities.

SPECIAL SKILLS AND ABILITIES

- Possess strong interpersonal communication skills, and have a demonstrated
  interest in working harmoniously with others
- Can organize own personal time and tasks efficiently
- Can present a professional company image to clients, fellow workers, and/or
  peers

BONDABLE: I am bondable, and can pass a police security check.

TRAVEL: Willing to comply with all travelling requirements; have own car.

SPECIAL TRAINING: Willing to undergo any amount of special training deemed necessary to more adequately meet the continuing demands of this position.

HOBBIES AND INTERESTS: meeting people; reading literature; physical fitness

AVAILABILITY: Immediate.

SALARY EXPECTED: Open — nature and challenge of position itself is of principal concern.

May 1991 - September 1991:   summer employment

    Department of Tourism
    43 Scenic Lane
    Carson City, Nevada

    <u>Tour Guide & Public Relations Person</u>: Principal duties and responsibilities
    involved the following: conducting guided tours for groups of tourists, the
    general public, and professional representatives of business and government;
    providing information on localities or attractions of special interest; an-
    swering the questions and concerns of tourists in a polite and professional
    manner, on matters pertaining to services and/or facilities in specific re-
    gions, etc.; preparing media kits and press releases; maintaining a bank of
    information on the times, dates, and locations of special events and activi-
    ties; providing slide shows, audio/video presentations, and lectures.

<u>BUSINESS REFERENCE</u>
Mr. Michael Wilson, Office Manager
Department of Tourism
43 Scenic Lane
Carson City, Nevada
Business telephone: (702) 885-4444

<u>CHARACTER REFERENCE</u>
Dr. Roy Hebert, Professor of Sociology
University of Nevada
76 Ivory Boulevard
Carson City, Nevada
Office telephone: (702) 885-0000

<u>ADDITIONAL REMARKS</u>: I am a results-oriented individual, and can work profit-
    ably, independently, or in cooperation with others; and I work with enthusi-
    asm and high energy on all assignments.

RESUME #52
SURVEYOR

Timothy L. Compass
95 Compass Crescent
Edmonton, Alberta
T5J 3A3

Home telephone: (403) 427-0000

EDUCATIONAL BACKGROUND

Civil Technology Diploma: Alberta Institute of Technology, Edmonton, Alberta, 1972

Diploma (Grade 12 Academic): City High School, Edmonton, Alberta, 1970

PROFESSIONAL AFFILIATIONS

(C.E.T.) Alberta Society of Certified Engineering Technicians & Technologists
(C.S.T.) Alberta Association of Certified Survey Technicians & Technologists

PROFESSIONAL EXPERIENCE

June 1972 - present
  Commercial Survey Limited
  9876 Riverside Drive
  Edmonton, Alberta

Survey Instrument Man, with the responsibility for:

WORKING ON SURVEYING PROJECTS that include: 1. Legal Surveys (i.e., Subdivisions, Property Line Agreements, Topographic, Retracements, Traverses, Monumentation for L.R.I.S., Building Location Surveys); 2. Layouts (i.e., Property and Building Corners); 3. Elevations (i.e., Photocontrol for L.R.I.S., Setting Grades, Bench Mark Circuits); 4. Survey Certificates; 5. Compass Lines; 6. Solar Observations;

MAKING COMPUTATIONS on Field Note Reductions, Subdivision Designs, Plotting Coordinate Points, Coordinate Geometry, Curves, Compass Rule and Transformation Adjustments;

OFFICE ADMINISTRATIVE DUTIES, such as writing Legal Survey Property Descriptions; doing Title Searches; property mapping; survey cost estimating; billing; and filing;

USING STANDARD DRAFTING INSTRUMENTS AND MATERIALS on Subdivisions and Survey Plans, Topographic & Plot Plans, and Property Identification Maps.

BUSINESS AND CHARACTER REFERENCES: Available Upon Request.

176

RESUME #53
SYSTEMS ANALYST

Victoria G. Datapac
321 Computer Boulevard
Indianapolis, IN 46204

Home telephone: (317) 232-1234

PERSONAL INFORMATION

Birth date: May 16, 1958
Marital status: single   Dependents: none

EDUCATIONAL BACKGROUND

Bachelor of Computer Science: University of Indianapolis, Indianapolis,
  Indiana, 1980

Diploma (Grade 12 Academic): Kennedy High School, Indianapolis, Indiana, 1976

KNOWLEDGE OF COMPUTER LANGUAGES: FORTRAN; PASCAL; C; COBOL; MACRO-ASSEMBLY;
  BASIC

KNOWLEDGE OF COMPUTER HARDWARE: IBM 3081; IBM 3083; IBM 3090

KNOWLEDGE OF COMPUTER APPLICATIONS: Accounting Programs; Lotus 1-2-3; Filing;
  Symphony; WordPerfect 5.0; Multiplan

KNOWLEDGE OF COMPUTER OPERATING SYSTEMS: MS DOS; MRX; VMS; Apple-Dos;
  CP/M; TRS-DOS; NOS; UNIX; MVS/XE; PC DOS

KNOWLEDGE OF DATA BASES: IDMS; DB2; dBase III; dBase III+; dBase IV;

PROFESSIONAL INTERESTS: keeping abreast of the ongoing changes, trends, and
  latest developments in state-of-the-art computer hardware and software

PROFESSIONAL EXPERIENCE

June 1980 - present: full-time employment
  United States Systems Ltd.
  1234 State Highway
  Indianapolis, Indiana

Systems Analyst for this international company which specializes in the sale
of cash registers and computers.

EXAMPLES OF SYSTEMS PERSONALLY DEVELOPED: point-of-sale terminals; on-line
DATAPAC to an IBM Series I front-end processor; credit authorization; data
collection; perpetual inventory system; after-hours polling via an NCR I-
9250 mini-computer to a VAX Mainframe on-line DATAPAC; data collection;
inter-store transfers; 35,000 item inventory system; batch communications
with BASIC FOUR Mainframe.
Reporting directly to the Systems Engineering Manager, specific duties and
responsibilities, in respect to the above mentioned systems, involve the following:

Developing Systems: Responsible for developing and implementing systems that would meet the requirements of the company's retail clients [i.e., developing, implementing, and maintaining information and control systems that provide timely and accurate information relating to operational efficiency to users (e.g., Performance Indicators, Evaluation Models, Data Base Management); working in close consultation with senior managers on the design and implementation of systems, processes and techniques; collaborating in the development, implementation and review of management tools such as Database Management and Operational Performance Measurement Systems; coordinating and monitoring the workflow in order to ensure that procedures are properly followed, schedules maintained, and objectives met; scheduling all production to ensure optimum usage of equipment (i.e., scheduling logs, re-run logs, security log, and incident log); ensuring that standard EDP security and backup procedures are properly in place];

Acting As A Liaison: Responsible for acting as a liaison between clients, Managers and company personnel in order to: **1.** present narrative and statistical reports on proposed changes to programs; **2.** evaluate the merits of programs being considered for implementation; **3.** establish guidelines; and **4.** integrate the collection of information and tasks; maintaining a liaison between customer departments in respect to control, balancing, and scheduling; consulting with Management Information Specialists for advice and guidance on the development and implementation of new systems;

Special Projects: Responsible for working on special projects when required by management (e.g., preparing test data for new production programs and verifying the results, etc.); preparing guides, tables, charts and various reports to assist users with their analysis and interpretation of output data; trouble-shooting problems encountered with hardware and software and advising technical experts of suspected problems.

ADDITIONAL REMARKS: I am a results-oriented individual, and can work profitably, independently, or in cooperation with others; and I work with enthusiasm and high energy on all assignments.

BUSINESS AND CHARACTER REFERENCES: Available Upon Request.

RESUME #54
TELEVISION DIRECTOR

Wanda N. Show
87 Hollywood Drive
Sacramento, CA 95814

Home telephone: (916) 324-1414

PERSONAL INFORMATION

Birth date: May 21, 1966
Marital status: single   Dependents: none

EDUCATIONAL BACKGROUND

Bachelor of Public Relations: University of Sacramento, Sacramento, California, 1989

Diploma (Grade 12 Academic): John D. High School, Sacramento, California, 1984

TELEVISION PROGRAMMING EXPERIENCE

September 1989 - present: full-time employment

    University of Sacramento
    Distant University Education Transmission (D.U.E.T.)
    Sacramento, California,

Director of an hour long live television program which provides educational lectures to its viewing audience, and is broadcast three times per week over local community television stations. Principal duties and responsibilities involve the following:

OVERSEEING TECHNICAL OPERATIONS: Responsible for overseeing all technical operations of educational broadcasts (i.e., determining the requirements for equipment such as microphones; cassette recorders; soundtrack intros, extros, and musical interludes; mixing console; telephone hybrid, etc.); operating and integrating all of the above mentioned equipment; interpreting and implementing broadcasting procedures desired by the Producer; ensuring technical excellence and adherence to sound professional practices in the recording and broadcasting of all programs, etc.; developing and maintaining good rapport and effective working relationships with the Producer, Technicians, Administrative Personnel, Production Staff, University Professors, and special guest speakers;

CAMERA OPERATIONS/AUDIO DUTIES: Responsible for operating television cameras during broadcasts, when required; video switching; adjusting and mixing sound during the taping of shows, as well as fitting the studio with the necessary audio equipment prior to broadcasts.

BUSINESS REFERENCES: Available Upon Request.

RESUME #55
TOURIST COUNSELOR

Albert K. Helpful
123 Advice Lane
Honolulu, HI 96813

Home telephone: (808) 548-7777

PERSONAL INFORMATION

Birth date: August 22, 1972
Health: excellent
Citizenship: American

EDUCATIONAL BACKGROUND

Diploma (Grade 12 Academic): Honolulu High School, Honolulu, Hawaii, 1990

HOBBIES AND INTERESTS: reading literature; physical fitness; meeting people

AVAILABILITY: Minimum of two weeks' notice required.

SUMMER EMPLOYMENT

June 1990 - present: full-time employment
  City of Honolulu
  (Department of Marketing & Promotions)
  774 Hastings Street
  Honolulu, Hawaii

Tourist Counselor. Reporting directly to the Supervisor on objectives and results, principal duties and responsibilities involve the following:

PUBLIC RELATIONS: Responsible for answering in a polite and professional manner inquiries, concerns, and/or complaints from tourists on matters pertaining to localities or attractions of special interest; promoting public awareness of the department through good public service;

OFFICE ADMINISTRATION: Responsible for maintaining a bank of information on
the times, dates, and locations of special events; preparing ongoing statistical reports on tourism patterns for the State of Hawaii; compiling and
evaluating data on tourism indicating tourism patterns in specific areas, localities or attractions of special interest, complaints or concerns of tourists respecting services and/or facilities in specific regions, etc.

BUSINESS AND CHARACTER REFERENCES: Available Upon Request.

RESUME #56
TRAVEL CONSULTANT

Yolande M. Tour
43 Scenic Drive
Edmonton, Alberta
T5J 3A3

Home telephone: (403) 427-0000

EDUCATIONAL BACKGROUND

Travel & Tourism Program: Edmonton Business College, Edmonton, Alberta, 1983
Diploma (Grade 12 Academic): Edmonton High School, Edmonton, Alberta, 1982

PROFESSIONAL EXPERIENCE

June 23, 1983 - January 1991: full-time employment
  Ulysses Travel Agency
  1133 St. George Boulevard
  Edmonton, Alberta

Travel Consultant for this local travel agency. Reporting directly to the Supervisor on business objectives and results, principal duties and responsibilities involved the following:

PUBLIC RELATIONS: Responsible for answering the inquiries of customers in a polite and professional manner; booking passenger reservations and ticketing; receiving customer payments in cash and/or credit card; working out various types of fares to ensure the most economical routes and advising customers on a variety of levels (i.e., high or low seasons; midweek or excursion fares; high, moderate or affordable tours; package tours; geography; health requirements; visas; rental cars; hotels; available recreational activities; theatre tickets; etc); arranging itineraries; booking airfares; developing effective working relationships with representatives of hotel chains and car rental companies, etc.; promoting public awareness of the company through good customer service;

COMPUTER OPERATIONS: Responsible for entering, retrieving, and analyzing data from the company's on-line computer; operating a RESERVEC System.

BUSINESS REFERENCE: Please see the enclosed letter of reference.

RESUME #57
TRUCK DRIVER

Brian G. Diesel
43 Tractor Drive
Atlanta, GA 30334

Home telephone: (404) 656-8000

PERSONAL INFORMATION

Birth date: May 19, 1955
Height: 5' 11"   Weight: 215 lbs.
Health: excellent
Physical handicaps: none
Citizenship: American
Georgia State driver's license number: 123456 (Class 1A Endorsement F)

EDUCATIONAL BACKGROUND

Straight Truck Driver Training Course, taken through Commercial Safety College,
   Atlanta, Georgia, 1974

Diploma (Grade 12 Academic): Elinor High School, Atlanta, Georgia, 1973

TRAVEL: Willing to comply with all travelling requirements; have own tractor
   trailer.

SHIFTWORK: Willing to work shiftwork.

OVERTIME: Willing to work any amount of overtime.

AVAILABILITY: Minimum of two weeks' notice required.

PROFESSIONAL EXPERIENCE

October 1974 – present: full-time employment
   Moncton Transport
   897 Hasting Street
   Atlanta, Georgia

Professional Truck Driver: Principal duties and responsibilities involve the
safe and efficient operation of a tractor trailer while transporting supplies to various points of destination throughout North America (i.e., operating diesel powered vehicles; practising safe driving techniques; rural
highway and urban driving; complying with vehicle inspection methods and procedures; providing basic mechanical work to tractor trailer, when required;
handling dangerous goods and supplies; maintaining weigh bills and bills of
lading; handling the inquiries and complaints of Shippers and Receivers in a
polite and professional manner).

BUSINESS REFERENCES: Available Upon Request.

182

RESUME #58
WAITRESS/BILINGUAL

Carla V. Kind
123 Main Street
Moncton, New Brunswick
E1B 3Y3

Home telephone: (506) 382-0000

PERSONAL INFORMATION

Health: excellent
Citizenship: Canadian
Social Insurance Number: 111 222 333

EDUCATIONAL BACKGROUND

Techniques d'Hôtellerie et de Restauration, New Brunswick Community College
   (Edmundston Campus), Edmundston, New Brunswick, 1982 - 1984

Diploma of Collegiate Studies (College d'Enseignement Général et Pro-
   fessionnel): Gaspé Peninsula College, Gaspé, Québec, 1982
   Major: Commerce

KNOWLEDGE OF LANGUAGES

<u>English</u>:
Speaking ability: excellent   Writing ability: excellent
Reading ability: excellent   Comprehension ability: excellent
<u>French</u>:
Speaking ability: excellent   Writing ability: excellent
Reading ability: excellent   Comprehension ability: excellent

SPECIAL SKILLS AND ABILITIES

- Possess strong interpersonal communication skills, and have a demonstrated interest in working harmoniously with others
- Can organize own personal time and tasks efficiently
- Can present a professional company image to customers, fellow workers, subordinates and/or peers

SHIFTWORK: Willing to work shiftwork.

OVERTIME: Willing to work any amount of overtime.

HOBBIES AND INTERESTS: meeting people; reading literature; physical fitness

AVAILABILITY: Minimum of two weeks' notice required.

SALARY EXPECTED: Open — nature and challenge of position itself is of principal concern.

WORK EXPERIENCE

June 1984 - present: full-time employment
  Hotel Richmond
  750 Gourmet Avenue
  Moncton, New Brunswick

Server for this national hotel, working in the dining room which has a seating capacity of approximately 40 - 45.

Reporting directly to the Maitre d', and working in both English and French, principal duties and responsibilities involve the following:

Acting In The Absence Of The Maitre d': Responsible for assuming total responsibility for the day-to-day routine operation of the dining room in the absence of the Maitre d', when required;

Public Relations: Responsible for serving hotel guests and the general public in a polite and professional manner; coordinating reservations in order to achieve maximum volume; receiving customer payments in cash and/or credit card; preparing and serving customer drinks; promoting public awareness of the hotel through the provision of good service to patrons.

SUMMER EMPLOYMENT

June 1982 - September 1982: summer employment
  Quinn's Restaurant
  21 Main Street
  Moncton, New Brunswick

Waitress for this family restaurant. Working in both official languages, principal duties were similar in nature to the Server position discussed in detail above.

BUSINESS AND CHARACTER REFERENCES: Available Upon Request.

RESUME #59
WELDER

David F. Mig
60 Weldon Avenue
Sudbury, Ontario
M7A 2H6

Home telephone: (416) 963-4444

PERSONAL INFORMATION

Marital status: single   Dependents: none
Height: 5' 11"   Weight: 175 lbs.
Health: excellent

EDUCATIONAL BACKGROUND

Have CSA Standard W47.1 (1983), Part I & Part II (SMAW, GMAW, FCAW, SAW, ESW)
  and CSA Standard W59 (1984)

Certificate of Qualification in Welding (T.Q.): issued by the Ontario Ministry
  of Labour, March 1984
  Note: Hold current status (F4 Qualified)

Welding Program: Ontario School of Trades and Technology, Toronto, Ontario,
  1983 - 1984

Diploma (Grade 12 Academic): Smith Community College, Toronto, Ontario, 1982

PROFESSIONAL INTERESTS: reading technical publications on welding; automotive
  repairs (i.e., body work and mechanical repairs)

AVAILABILITY: Minimum of two weeks' notice required.

PROFESSIONAL EXPERIENCE

June 1984 - present: full-time employment
  Pulp & Paper Canada Ltd.
  1234 Cedar Avenue
  Sudbury, Ontario

Welder: Reporting directly to the Foreman, principal duties and responsibilities involve serving as a troubleshooter to assess the type of welding repair work and installations required (i.e., damage repairs, metal replacements, restoration, material, time requirements and equipment needed, etc.);
performing detailed component part inspections; operating Mig Welding Equipment, a Hydraulic Press, Stationary, Mobile, and Multiple Drills, Grinders,
Shapers, Oxy-Acetylene Tables, Hydraulic Cutters and Huck Machines; practising good housekeeping standards in order to ensure the occupational health
and safety of all on-site workers.

BUSINESS REFERENCE: Available Upon Request.

OTHER TITLES IN THE SELF-COUNSEL SERIES

ASSERTIVENESS FOR MANAGERS
Learning effective skills for managing people
by Diana Cawood, B.A., M.Sc.

Good communication has always been the key to good management in large and small businesses. Now, the assertive skills so widely used in personal relationships can be transeferred to the workplace to facilitate staff communication, improve morale, and increase productivity.

During the past decade, employee attitudes about work and authority have changed dramatically. A manager today can no longer rely on old methods of management. Modern managers need to learn the basic skills of assertive behavior as applied in business organizations. This book takes a fresh, step-by-step approach to developing assertive skills in a variety of work settings. Individual exercises can be used to apply the principles discussed to your own situation. $12.95

This book answers such questions as:

- Does assertiveness always work? Is it sometimes necessary to revert to old-fashioned methods?

- Can you be yourself and still get ahead?

- How do you handle a problem employee?

- When and how do you help an employee with career planning?

- How do you respond to unreasonable demands from your own superior?

- What do you do when the other person is being assertive too?

- What is the assertive way to respond to criticism?

- What are the special concerns for women managers?

THE FIRST-TIME MANAGER: A SURVIVAL GUIDE
by Theodore G. Tyssen

Learning to lead can be a rocky, prolonged ordeal for the freshly promoted manager. There are no quick-fix, one-minute solutions to supervising a team and boosting productivity.

"The professional practice of managing people is as challenging and complex as the practice of law or medicine," says Theodore Tyssen. Tyssen speaks from experience, having parachuted into his first managerial position 30 years ago with only a scant understanding of the people managing responsibilities involved with the new job. Since that time, he has seen a generation of new managers long on technical expertise but short on leadership skills struggle with the problems of establishing themselves in a supervisory role. His practical, down-to-earth guide helps new recruits cultivate a competent and confident managerial style, one that improves team morale and bumps up the bottom line.

This book explores the five fundamental processes that every well-rounded, effective team manager must understand and use. It shows how to select the right people for the job, provide orientation and direction, design a productive work environment, train and develop skills, and motivate today's staff. Moreover, the book supports the flexible, team-oriented management style which is revolutionizing the workplace in the 90s.

The leap from worker to manager is the most important step and biggest change in a career. This book is for the newly minted manager who wants to avoid a trial by fire and make the move to management a positive and productive one for everyone concerned. $7.95

THE BUSINESS GUIDE TO EFFECTIVE SPEAKING
Making presentations, using audio-visuals, and dealing with the media
by Jacqueline Dunckel and Elizabeth Parnham

When you are called upon to speak in front of your business colleagues, or asked to represent your company in front of the media, do you communicate your thoughts effectively? Or do you become tongue-tied, nervous, and worry about misrepresenting yourself and your business?

Effective communication has always been the key to business success and this book provides a straightforward approach to developing techniques to improve your on-the-job speaking skills. This book is as easy to pick up and use as a quick reference for a specific problem as it is to read from cover to cover. Whether you want to know how to deal with the media, when to use visual aids in a presentation, or how to prepare for chairing a meeting, this book will answer your questions and help you regain your confidence. $7.95

Some of the questions it answers are:
- Should I speak from notes or from a prepared script?
- Is it all right to tell a joke?
- What do I do to improve my voice?
- Which visual aids work best?
- How do I overcome nervousness?
- How do I handle hostile questions from the audience?
- How do I stay in control when I'm being interviewed?
- What should I wear to speak on television?
- When should teleconferencing be used?

PRACTICAL TIME MANAGEMENT
How to get more things done in less time
by Bradley C. McRae

Here is sound advice for anyone who needs to develop practical time management skills. It is designed to help any busy person, from any walk of life, use his or her time more effectively. Not only does it explain how to easily get more things done, it shows you how your self-esteem will improve in doing so. More important, emphasis is placed on maintenance so that you remain in control. Whether you want to find extra time to spend with your family or read the latest bestseller, this book will give you the guidance you need — without taking up a lot of your time! $6.95

Some of the skills you will learn are:
- Learning to monitor where your time goes
- Setting realistic and attainable goals
- Overcoming inertia
- Rewarding yourself
- Planning time with others
- Managing leisure time
- Planning time for hobbies and vacations
- Maintaining the new you

KEEPING TRACK
An organizer for your legal, business, and personal records

The key to being in control of your personal affairs is knowing where everything is.

This book helps you gather all the information concerning your personal affairs so that, by yourself or with the help of professionals, you can plot legal and investment strategies. The information it contains on the legal and tax implications of decisions will help you become a more informed consumer of professional services.

By completing this book, you will relieve your family of the burden of locating all the information to administer your affairs if you should die.

Some of the areas covered include:

- Sharing information with your spouse or partner
- Dividing your assets
- Business concerns
- Understanding and preserving your assets
- Debts and liabilities

Canadian edition
by Jack J. Shaffer, CLU, CH.F.C., and
Martin D. Zlotnick, B.Comm., LL.B.
$12.95

U.S. edition
by Ann Kruse, Attorney, $10.95

Also available:
THE KEEPING TRACK CASE
A sturdy, multi-pocketed accordion file for organizing and protecting your important papers. ($12.95 in Canada, $10.95 in U.S.)

THE KEEPING TRACK PAK
The Keeping Track guide and case conveniently packaged and shrink-wrapped; offered at a reduced price. $24.95
